"[Nico Castel] is a musical resource to all of us. This book indispensable tools for singers and teachers." — **Rita Shane**, Soprano, Metropolitan Opera, and Professor of Voice, Eastman School of Music

"What Nico Castel brings to his work is not only a solution to the problem at hand or a set of rules to memorize. Nico goes further to ignite the spark of curiosity which changes the way one works from that moment on. Surely he merits the title of Language and Diction Guru. Bravo, Nico!" — **Frank Lopardo**, Tenor, Metropolitan Opera

"From Nico Castel — great artist, teacher and friend — one can only expect the best. His energy, vast experience, excellence and good humor are invaluable assets in a teacher, and my admiration for him has no limits." — **Veronica Vallarroel**, Soprano, Metropolitan Opera

"The guidance and instruction from Nico Castel early in my career have proven to be the most substantial and valued contributions to my performance preparation." — **Robert Hale**, Bass-baritone, Metropolitan Opera

"Nico's brilliant new book should be the reference book of the century for aspiring opera singers and opera lovers everywhere." — **Judith Blegen**, Soprano, Metropolitan Opera

"In the course of my developing career, I can say with enormous confidence that whatever linguistic proficiency I have, I owe to Nico Castel. Thanks, Nico, for unlocking some of these mysteries for us!" — **Susan Graham**, Mezzo-soprano, Metropolitan Opera

"I had the great honor and privilege to work with Nico Castel while in the Met's Young Artist program. His wealth of knowledge never ceases to amaze me and his help has been, and continues to be, invaluable." — **Dwayne Croft**, Baritone, Metropolitan Opera

"Nico Castel has served as a supporting and informative teacher to me. Thank you, Nico." — **Renée Fleming,** Soprano, Metropolitan Opera

"There is no doubt that I would not be where I am today if it had not been for the invaluable assistance of Nico Castel." — **Eric Halfvarson**, Bass, Metropolitan Opera

"Nico works with a singer beyond the rules of proper articulation. He teaches the nuance and rich coloration found in the words of the language that helps each artist discover a more expressive foundation for interpretation." — **Judith Christin**, Mezzo-soprano, Metropolitan Opera

"For many years, I have been a great admirer of Nico Castel. Theory and practice are wonderfully balanced in his teaching. He has been an integral and consistent source of reliable, practical information to professionals for decades. He has a well-integrated approach to phonetics that gives the serious student invaluable tools with which to develop." — **Hal France**, Conductor, New York City Opera Company

"My development with Nico Castel's guidance has been as important and helpful to my career as my studies in any other areas. He adjusts his comments with each singer individually and carefully so as not to disturb either the correctness of phonetic sound or the technical intricacies of the singing process. He brings a special passion and love to his art — one is immediately taken, even enthralled, with his special flair." — **Mark Oswald**, Baritone, Metropolitan Opera

"The preparation of a role in my repertoire is never complete without my work with Nico Castel. Style is founded in language, and for me, both are personified in one man: Nico Castel." — **Frances Ginsberg**, Soprano, Metropolitan Opera

"I can't think of anyone more qualified to author [this book] than Nico Castel, with his remarkable command of languages and all of their nuances. His assistance has been invaluable to me for all of my roles." — **James Morris**, Bass-baritone, Metropolitan Opera

"Nico Castel continues to be one of the most important influences on my professional life. In his studio I have learned the phonetics and rules of the languages and much more. [He] ties all the elements together in a way that anyone can understand." — **Kevin Murphy**, Coach/accompanist, Metropolitan Opera

"Nico Castel has been one of the treasures in my preparation for a career in singing. He has a beautiful way of explaining the intricacies of a language that can be easily understood and applied. As an American singer, I feel confident in the international world of singing, thanks in large part to Nico Castel." — **Heidi Grant Murphy**, Soprano, Metropolitan Opera

"My esteemed friend and colleague, Nico Castel, is a brilliant master of many languages." — **Gary Lakes**, Tenor, Metropolitan Opera

NICO CASTEL

A Singer's Manual of Spanish Lyric Diction

FOREWORD BY PLÁCIDO DOMINGO

Excalibur Publishing
New York

Published by:
Excalibur Publishing
434 Avenue of the Americas, Suite 790
New York, New York 10011

Cover design: Kara Glasgold, Griffin Design
Illustrations: Arlene Weinstein
Musical examples: Brian Schexnayder

Library of Congress Cataloging in Publication Data

Castel, Nico.
    A singer's manual of Spanish lyric diction / Nico Castel :
foreword by Plácido Domingo.
        p.   cm.
    Includes bibliographical references (p.) and index.
    ISBN 0-9627226-9-3 (paperback)
    1. Singing–Diction. 2. Spanish language–Pronunciation.
I. Title.
MT883.C27   1994
783'.043–dc20   94-6333
                                                  CIP
                                                  MN

Printed in the United States of America

10 9 8 7 6 5 4 3 2 1

I lovingly dedicate this book to my wife, Carol, without whose vision, hard work, infinite patience and encouragement, it would never have become a reality; and also to the memory of my father, Felix, who was the true linguist in the family.

CONTENTS

Acknowledgments

I wish to sincerely thank the following persons for their invaluable support and assistance, without which this book could never have been written: Scott Wiley, Carole and C.J. Everett, Jairo Nomicón, James Courtney, Jane Gottlieb, Carleton Sprague Smith, Maria Ciaccia, Eugene Green, Suzann Dvorken, Plácido Domingo, Millie Grant, Geri Thoma, Evan Bjornen and Luis Gutierrez. A special thanks to my daughter, Sasha, for her splendid ideas, and to my dear friend and colleague, Brian Schexnayder, a "mil gracias" for all his invaluable assistance, super-human patience and advice with computers.

FOREWORD

Spanish music has always played a great part in my life. From my tenderest childhood years, I was immersed in it. My parents were both performers in zarzuela, and I have listened to this beautiful music all through my childhood and adulthood.

Throughout my career, I have always enjoyed singing the music of my heritage, be it songs of Spain or Latin America. From the *Cantigas* of Alfonso el Sabio in the thirteenth century, through the intervening centuries to the music of today, there is a vast wealth of beautiful Spanish vocal music.

My long-time friend and colleague, Nico Castel, has written a book that is indispensible to the English-speaking singer wishing to acquire the skills necessary to sing in Spanish. First and foremost, it addresses the Castillian idiom, but it also explores the Latin American variants needed to sing music from the New World.

Nico has written an eminently useful book, and it is my sincere wish that it will help stimulate interest in the music of my heritage.

Plácido Domingo
New York, 1993

1

PREFACE

I have written this book to bring the wealth of Spanish vocal music and the English-speaking singer together. It is designed to help the singer acquire the necessary diction skills to make his singing as authentic and idiomatic as possible. It will explain the necessary vowel sounds and consonant articulation required to be able to sing in Spanish without betraying any of the common faults of English-speaking singers, who are used to the aspirated consonants and diphthongized vowel sounds of their language. Although "Spanish," as defined in this book, is the classic Castillian pronunciation as it is spoken today in Spain, Latin American variant forms will also be discussed, so that repertoire from this hemisphere can be sung authentically as well.

For those of you who have no knowledge of, or are only generally familiar with, the International Phonetic Alphabet (IPA), don't let the symbols and technical words intimidate you. It is really quite easy to digest with a little attention and reduces foreign language pronunciation to one simple, reliable, universally understood code.

It has been said that Italian is the optimal language for singing, due to its long, accented vowels and the relatively high ratio of vowels to consonants, its legato articulation, the total absence of glottal stops, and lack of aspiration in its plosive consonants. In many ways, Spanish is as singable a language as its sister Romance language. It links its phrases, as Italian does, and there are no glottal stops as in German or English. In certain instances, Spanish is even more singable than Italian, in that interior consonants (that is, consonants that are not absolutely initial in a word or group of words), such as [b], [d] and [g], are softened to [β], [ð] and [ɣ]. Even considering that all plurals are formed by adding an *s* (as in English and contrary to Italian, which forms its plurals by changing the end vowel), this factor does not add sibilance to the sung language. This is because this final *s* in plurals, in many cases, softens to almost a [z] sound through

3

assimilation with the voiced consonants that follow in the word group or breath phrase (See Chapter 9 — Assimilation).

The consonant clusters with the letter *r*, such as *cr, pr, tr* and *fr,* are much less vibrant than their Italian cousins. For instance, the Italian word *credo* (I believe) is pronounced with a true rolled [r], whereas its Spanish counterpart, *creo,* is pronounced with a mere flipped [ɾ], or [ˈkɾeɔ]. Likewise, in such pairs as Italian *proteggimi* and Spanish *protégeme,* or Italian *freddo* and Spanish *frío,* the Spanish words have a greatly reduced energy on the *r.* There are no such initial consonant clusters in Spanish as in the Italian *spr* of *spremere, str* of *strepito,* or *scr* of *scrivere.* The comparable words in Spanish add an *e* at the beginning of these words, thus: *esprimir, estrépito* and *escribir.* One could say that these Spanish words, having that extra vowel at the beginning, are more singable than their Italian counterparts, by virtue of having an extra vowel to sing on and a greatly reduced vibrant *r* in the consonant cluster.

Spoken Castillian Spanish has very crisp, short vowels, which may prompt some to call it a "staccato" language. When compared to its sister language, Italian, which has long stressed vowels, one must concede that. However, sung Spanish loses that staccato quality, because when the words are set to music, the process immediately elongates the sounds of the words, and the language becomes as legato as any other.

Since the singing process will homogenize many vowel sounds of minute variation, we will provide the singer with an uncomplicated Spanish vowel system consisting of five comfortable sounds for singing.

This book will not deal with phrasal cadence or speech intonation — a subject necessary for speaking, but not singing. Singers have the benefit of the musical line to guide them. For singers needing to speak lines, a dialogue coach is recommended.

CHAPTER 1

An Introduction to Spanish Vocal Music

Spanish vocal music is the sadly forgotten repertoire. When American singers think of Spanish music, they immediately name the de Falla songs, some Granados *Tonadillas*, the Obradors and Nin arrangement collections, perhaps some Turina songs, and maybe the *Cuatro Madrigales Amatorios* of Joaquín Rodrigo. What singers do not know is that there is a vast, beautifully noble and haunting wealth of old Spanish music going back to the thirteenth century that is rarely performed, simply because people do not know of its existence. In my Spanish Vocal Repertoire courses, I have tried to remedy this by supplying participants with copies of this rare and mostly unobtainable music for their own collections, and I must say that I have been much gratified to see many of my students begin to include some of this repertoire in their recital programs.

Throughout musical history, Spain has held a fascination for composers of many lands, and many have looked westward beyond the Pyrenees for their inspiration: Bizet, Glinka, Tchaikovsky, Debussy, Chabrier, Lalo, Liszt, Rimsky-Korsakoff, Verdi (in his Moorish "Canzon del Velo" in Act II of *Don Carlo*) and others.

Spanish song dates back to antiquity. The Iberian peninsula was first populated by the Iberians, then the Greeks, Carthaginians, Romans, Visigoths and Moors, in that order. Records from as early as the Greek domination show that young maidens accompanied their singing with castanets. Rome governed the peninsula for six centuries until A.D. 476. Then after the fall of Rome, the Visigoths and Christianity dominated in the land until the arrival of the Islamic Moors in A.D. 711. The historical events that helped shape Spain also influenced Spanish music as we recognize it today.

The Moors invaded Spain from the north coast of Africa and advanced slowly northward, occupying the peninsula almost in its entirety, except for some northern Cantabric pockets, where the germ of a "reconquest" began almost immediately. It took eight hundred years for this reconquest to finally achieve its goal: the expulsion of the Moors, "the hated infidel," from Spanish soil. Christian fervor was running high, and Moors, Jews and all other non-Christians were forced to leave Spain by the dreaded Spanish Inquisition. They were given the option of conversion to Christianity, death at the stake or outright expulsion. The Sephardic or Spanish Jews, who for so many centuries had enjoyed their "golden age" in Spain, were forced to leave their homeland, taking with them their language (the Spanish of the time) and their songs into a long and unknown diaspora.

This eight-hundred-year occupation by the Moors ended in 1492 (the same year as the first trip by Christopher Columbus) with the reconquest of Granada by the Catholic kings Ferdinand of Aragón and Isabella of Castille. These eight hundred years of Moorish dominance left a living testament of Islamic art and architecture. It is the cities of Seville, Córdoba and Granada that are considered the crowning jewels of Moorish architectural and artistic achievement. The Moors also left their mark on Spanish music, namely the Oriental melisma and modal cadences which are so easily recognized in the Cante Jondo (Flamenco singing), with its throaty and inimitable style. It is truly amazing how similar the singing of a true Flamenco *cantaor* is to the chants of an Islamic muezzin calling the faithful to prayers from his perch atop a minaret.

Alfonso the Wise, known as "El Sabio" (1221-1284), ruled in a court that loved the arts and music. He and his disciples wrote over four hundred songs in praise of the Virgin Mary *(Cantigas de Santa Maria)*, extolling her miracles and good deeds. It must be understood that Moorish dominance was never a harsh, autocratic rule. It tolerated Islam, Judaism and Christianity alike. But by the thirteenth century, anti-Moorish sentiment was running high, and Alfonso's *Cantigas* were created in a strong burst of Christian fervor. The reconquest was fully underway. The *Cantigas* were found by modern

Spanish scholars in this century and transcribed from the original neumes into modern notation. They are written in *Gallego* (Galician), the classical language of poetry at the time. This language eventually became the language of Galicia, the northwestern province of Spain. The official language of the rest of Spain (except Catalonia and the Basque provinces) became *Castellano* (Castillian). From *Gallego* evolved Portuguese, a close linguistic cousin, which was to become the language of the other occupant of the Iberian Peninsula.

The court of Ferdinand and Isabella boasted many poet-musicians who wrote for the voice using the *villancico,* or rustic poem, as their base. This *villancico* was in Spain what the madrigal was for the rest of Europe. Another song form was the "romance," or ballad, mostly derived from the epics of chivalry (the same chivalry books or *libros de caballerías* which drove poor Don Quijote insane). Whereas the lute was the favored stringed instrument of the Moors and the rest of sixteenth century Europe, the Spanish rejected the Moorish instrument, which perhaps reminded them of the hated Islamic subjugation, and instead fashioned the vihuela, the stringed instrument which was to become the ancestor of the modern Spanish guitar. As Donald Henahan of *The New York Times* amusingly wrote on Wednesday, October 20, 1971:

> "Like the Swoose, which is neither Swan nor Goose, the Spanish vihuela was neither lute nor guitar. Womanly in shape, the 16th century plucked instrument spoke as women in myth and legend speak, softly and modestly. It was double strung, like the European lute, and usually tuned similarly. It died around 1600, possibly of acute confusion."

Many composers of the sixteenth century wrote for the voice with vihuela accompaniment. Luys Milán, Narvaez, Mudarra, Valderrábano, Morales and Fuenllana are just a few of the names associated with this fertile period of vocal composition in Spain. We can be eternally thankful to that most distinguished Spanish singer of the golden voice, Victoria de los Angeles, for having left us a priceless recorded legacy of this wonderful repertoire, which spans these five centuries of Spanish music.

Many of these *villancicos* and romances were written about Moorish subjects and were called *villancicos moriscos*. These include the well-known, anonymous "Tres Moricas m'enamoran en Jaén" ("Three Moorish Girls Enchant Me in Jaén"), and "Paseábase el rey Moro" ("The Moorish King Was Strolling"), by Luys de Narvaez (sixteenth century), in which the Moorish king, as he strolls through Granada, is brought news of the capture of the city of Alhama.

The zarzuela was to become Spain's own musical theater form. The first known zarzuela was performed at (and acquired its name from) the Teatro de la Zarzuela, outside Madrid, named for the bramble bushes, or *zarzas,* outside. It has music, dance, spoken dialogue, orchestral music — a little of everything, or *un poco de todo,* as they say in Spanish. (No wonder a Spanish culinary delicacy called *zarzuela* was invented: a concoction of seafood, soup, sausages — also *un poco de todo!)* The first zarzuela was performed in 1657, and from then until now, except for a period of about a hundred years when it was eclipsed by Italian opera, has reigned supreme in Spanish favor.

The "Italian invasion" happened in the eighteenth century, when such well-known composers as Domenico Scarlatti and Luigi Boccherini settled in Spain. The famous castrato, Carlo Broschi, better known as Farinelli, was brought to Spain, given a princely salary, and set up in great splendor in his own palace. The ruling monarch at the time, Philip V, suffered from acute melancholia, and only Farinelli's soothing virtuoso singing could relieve His Majesty's suffering. Although most of the music in this period of Spanish musical history sounds like the late baroque or early classical style of Haydn, Pergolesi and Cimarosa, the infectious Spanish rhythms of the *seguidilla, jota, farruca* and *fandango* can be heard permeating some of the compositions of the time. In subsequent years, other Spanish dance rhythms such as the *bolero, sevillana,* the Catalonian *sardana* and the Basque *zortzico* are to be found animating music of that period.

The nineteenth and twentieth centuries produced composers who truly established a Spanish style of music: de Falla, Granados, Albéniz, Turina, Rodrigo, Truán, Toldrá, Bacarisse, Osma, Arambarri, Leoz, Abril, Martinez-Palomo and others. A partial listing of vocal music by these and other composers is included in Appendix B. Latin America amalgamated some of the Spanish style and mixed it with Amerindian (Indians from the Americas) and African rhythms and motifs to create a vast array of song, both in a popular and classical vein. The Spanish language also underwent some changes after its ocean crossing, which will be discussed in Chapter 11 — Latin American Variants.

The Judeo-Spanish, or Ladino, language of the Sephardic or Spanish Jews is covered in Chapter 12, and it is included in this book because of the increasingly popular, and now eminently available, repertoire of these hauntingly beautiful songs — ever so melismatic, evoking shades of an ancient Orientalism which is truly exotic. The Spanish language is very singable, and the available repertoire, both for the lighter-voiced concert singer and the more robust operatic type, is there for the picking. Because of its popular origins and nationalistic identity, zarzuela singing should never be confused with "operetta-like" singing. Some zarzuela arias require the robustness of a *Tosca* Domingo-type tenor, others the agility of a full lyric soprano who can safely manage the demands of Leonora's arias from *Il Trovatore*.

It is my sincere wish that this book will stimulate the singer to explore the available possibilities in this beautiful and generally little-known repertory.

CHAPTER 2

Spanish Pronunciation

The generally-recognized standard for good Spanish pronunciation is Castillian *(Castellano)*, which is spoken by both cultivated people and peasants of Castille. In fact, they are the historical originators of the language in its purest form, and are perhaps, even today, its chief guardian. It is the language taught in schools and used by actors, singers and all involved in the pedagogic scene. It eschews all vulgarisms found in local dialects and certain pedantic exaggerations that can be found among overzealous speakers.

The chart on the following pages outlines the Spanish letters and their varying sounds using the International Phonetic Alphabet (IPA) symbols. Examples are given in English when possible, and when not, appropriate examples are given in other languages with which singers are certainly acquainted.

Some Characteristic Spanish Sounds

While the following chapters will cover Spanish vowels and consonants in greater depth, it is useful to have an overview of several sounds particularly characteristic of the Spanish language.

Examples of English sounds are given where possible, so that a person with no knowledge of other languages can get an approximate idea of what the Spanish sound is. Since it is almost impossible to render some of the Spanish sounds with an exact English equivalent, and since most singers have an acquaintance with Italian, German or French, examples in those languages are also given, when applicable, to help the singer better understand.

SPANISH LETTERS AND PHONETIC SOUNDS

LETTER	IPA	POSITION IN WORD	SPANISH EXAMPLE	SPANISH IPA	OTHER EXAMPLES
a	[a]	in all positions	agua, mano	[aɣwa], [mano]	Ital: caro, casa
b	[b]	in absolute initial position	banco	[baŋko]	Eng: bill Ital: bene
	[b]	after *m*	ambos	[ambɔs]	Eng: combine Colloq Ger: schwimmen [ʃβɪmɛn]
	[β]	in interior position	hablar, el barco	[aβlar], [ɛlβarko]	
c	[θ]*	before *e* and *i*	Cecilia	[θɛθilja]	Eng: thing, thumb
	[k]**	before *a, o, u*	caracol, cuna	[karakɔl], [kuna]	Eng: cake Ital: casa, come, culla

*In Latin America, the letter *c* before *e* and *i* is pronounced as a simple [s]. Ex: Cecilia [sesilja]
**The hard *c* [k] must be unaspirated.

LETTER	IPA	POSITION IN WORD	SPANISH EXAMPLE	SPANISH IPA	OTHER EXAMPLES
ch	[tʃ]	in all positions	muchacho, chorro	[mutʃatʃɔ], [tʃɔrrɔ]	Eng: chimney, champ
d	[d]	in absolute initial position	dolor, doña	[dolor], [doɲa]	Eng: door, dime Ital: dammi
	[d]	after *n*	donde, lindo	[dondɛ], [lindɔ]	Eng: tender
	[d]	after *l*	tilde, celda	[tildɛ], [θɛlda]	Eng: seldom

LETTER	IPA	POSITION IN WORD	SPANISH EXAMPLE	SPANISH IPA	OTHER EXAMPLES
d (cont.)	[ð]	in interior position (except after *n* or *l*)	nada, los dedos	[naða], [lɔzðeðɔs]	Eng: this, that
e	[ɛ]	in all positions	elefante	[ɛlefante]	Eng: well Ital: bella
f	[f]	in all positions	fábula, refresco	[faβula], [refreskɔ]	Eng: fit, frank
g	[g]	in initial position before *a, o, u*	gato, gota, gusto	[gatɔ], [gɔta], [gustɔ]	Ital: galante, gola Eng: gate, goat, good Ger: Bach, Buch
	[x]	before *e, i*	genio, gitano	[xɛnjɔ], [xitanɔ]	No example available; not used in other languages.
	[ɣ]	in interior position before *a, o, u*	haga, luego, agudo	[aɣa], [lweɣɔ], [aɣuðɔ]	
	[ɣ]	in other interior positions	desgracia, el gato, la gota	[dezɣraθja], [ɛlɣatɔ], [laɣɔta]	
	[g]	spelled *gue* and *gui* in initial position	guerra, guitarra	[gɛrra], [gitarra]	Eng: guess, guilt
	[ɣ]	spelled *gue* and *gui* in interior position	aguerrido, águila	[aɣɛrriðɔ], [aɣila]	Fr: baguette, déguisement
	[g]	after nasal [ŋ]	bilingüe, lingüistica	[bilingwe], [lingwistika]	Eng: hunger
h	SILENT		hogar, hablar	[ɔɣar], [aβlar]	Ital: ho, hai, hanno

In Latin America, the [x] sound of *j* and *g* (before *e* and *i*) would be softened to a pronounced [h].

i	[i]	in all positions	isla, fila, maní	[izla], [fila], [mani]	Ital: vino, così Eng: bee, seem
	[ja]	as on-glide	piano	[pjanɔ]	Ital: pianta
	[je]	as on-glide	tiene	[tjene]	Ital: pieno
	[jɔ]	as on-glide	adiós	[aðjɔs]	Ital: piove
	[ju]	as on-glide	viuda	[bjuða]	Ital: fiume
	[aj]	as off-glide	baile	[bajlɛ]	Ital: mai
	[ɛj]	as off-glide	peine	[pejne]	Ital: lei
	[ɔj]	as off-glide	boina	[bojna]	Ital: poi
	[uj]	as off-glide	cuitada	[kujtaða]	Ital: lui
j	[x]	initial and interior	jóven, majo	[xoβen], [maxɔ]	Ger: Bach, Buch
k	[k]	Not really a Spanish letter. Used only in foreign names and words.	kilómetro, wisky	[kilɔmetrɔ], [wiskɪ]	Eng: kill
l	[l]	in all positions	litro, alto, mil	[litrɔ], [altɔ], [mil]	Ital: molto, fila

In Spanish, we use the alveolar [l]. English examples are not given, because in American speech, we use the "dark" [ł], which cannot be used in Spanish. Therefore, only Italian examples are given.

LETTER	IPA	POSITION IN WORD	SPANISH EXAMPLE	SPANISH IPA	OTHER EXAMPLES
ll	[ʎ]	initial and interior	llorar, Sevilla	[ʎoɾaɾ], [seβiʎa]	Ital: figlio, moglie

In Latin America, the [j] is mostly used, or its close alternates, the [dj] or [dʒ] affricate sounds. The word for *horse*, *caballo*, would be pronounced in Mexico and most of Central America as [kaβajɔ]. In the rest of Latin America, we hear [kaβadjɔ] or [kaβadʒɔ], and in the River Plate estuary of Argentina and Uruguay, [kaβaʒɔ] or even [kaβaʃɔ]. (See Chapter 11 — Latin American Variants.)

LETTER	IPA	POSITION IN WORD	SPANISH EXAMPLE	SPANISH IPA	OTHER EXAMPLES
m	[m]	initial and interior	mano, amanecer	[manɔ], [amaneθeɾ]	Eng: man, omen
n	[n]	initial, interior, final	nana, mano, fin	[nana], [manɔ], [fin]	Eng: name, man
	[m]	before bilabial *m* by assimilation*	inmemorable, un momento	[immemoɾaβle], [ummɔmentɔ]	Ital: con moto
	[m]	before other bilabials (*p* and *b*) by assimilation*	un beso, un poco	[umbesɔ], [umpɔkɔ]	Ital: un poema, un bacio
	[ɱ]	before labiodental *f* by assimilation*	infierno, un favor	[imfjeɾnɔ], [uɱfaβɔɾ]	Ital: infatti, un filo
	[ŋ]	before velar consonants [k], [g], [x]	cinco, sangre, enjambre	[θiŋkɔ], [saŋgɾe], [eŋxambɾe]	Eng: think, bang; Ital: cinque, sangue

*See Chapter 9 — Assimilation. Italian examples are given, because the assimilation phenomenon also occurs in Italian; it does not occur in well-spoken English.

LETTER	IPA	POSITION IN WORD	SPANISH EXAMPLE	SPANISH IPA	OTHER EXAMPLES
ñ	[ɲ]	initial and interior	ñato, español	[ɲatɔ], [espaɲɔl]	Eng: canyon; Ital: sogno

o	[ɔ]	in all positions	otro, potro	[ɔtrɔ], [pɔtrɔ]	British: pot, got Ital: cosa, sposa
p	[p]	initial and interior	paño, aprender	[paɲɔ], [aprendɛr]	Eng: pit, paper Ital: potere, disposto

The Spanish *p*, like its Italian cousin, is unaspirated.

q	[k]	spelled *qui* and *que* in initial and interior positions	quiso, aquel, quitar, querer, inquilino	[kisɔ], [akɛl], [kitar], [kɛrɛr], [iŋkilinɔ]	Eng: quiche, keg, mosquito Fr: querelle, laquelle

As with the hard *c*, this sound must be unaspirated. The *que* and *qui* combinations are **not** pronounced as in Italian, [kwɛ] and [kwi].

r	[r]	in initial position (rolled)	rojo, ramo	[rɔxɔ], [ramɔ]	British: red Ital: raggio
	[r]	after *s, n, l* (rolled)	Israel, alrededor, enrojecer, en rumbo	[izraɛl], [alrɛðɛðɔr], [ɛnrɔxɛθɛr], [ɛnrumbɔ]	British: is right, on red
	[r]	before consonant (rolled)	parte, corte	[partɛ], [kɔrtɛ]	Ital: porta, carta
	[r]	as final (rolled)	amar, cantar	[amar], [kantar]	Ital: cor
	[ɾ]	after all other consonants except *s, n* or *l* (flipped)	prestar, crear, adrede, abreviar, frio, grande, treinta	[prestar], [krear], [aðrɛðɛ], [aβrɛβjar], [friɔ], [grandɛ], [treinta]	British: present, fragile

LETTER	IPA	POSITION IN WORD	SPANISH EXAMPLE	SPANISH IPA	OTHER EXAMPLES
r (cont.)	[ɾ]	between vowels (flipped)	era, cara, mira	[ɛɾa], [kaɾa], [miɾa]	Ital: amore
rr	[rr]	interior positions only	carro, horror	[karro], [ɔrror]	Ital: terrore
s	[s]	initial, interior, final	solo, salsa, jamás	[solɔ], [salsa], [xamas]	Eng: soul, salad
	[s]	between vowels	casa, cosa	[kasa], [kɔsa]	Eng: case
	[z]	before voiced consonants in a word or word group by assimilation	mismo, desde, muslo, los besos, mis labios	[mizmɔ], [dezðe], [muzlɔ], [lɔzβesɔs], [mizlaβjɔs]	Ital: sdegno, smania
t	[t]	initial and interior	tonto, batata	[tontɔ], [batata]	Ital: tutto, tanto

The Spanish *t* **must** be unaspirated. For that reason, no English example is given.

LETTER	IPA	POSITION IN WORD	SPANISH EXAMPLE	SPANISH IPA	OTHER EXAMPLES
u	[u]	initial and interior	uno, fortuna	[unɔ], [fɔrtuna]	Ital: luna, mula Eng: boom, zoom
	[wa]	as on-glide	cuatro	[kwatrɔ]	Ital: quasi Eng: quart
	[wɛ]	as on-glide	huevo	[weβɔ]	Ital: questo Eng: quest
	[wi]	as on-glide	huida	[wiða]	Ital: qui Eng: quit
	[wɔ]	as on-glide	quota	[kwɔta]	Ital: cuore Eng: quote
v	[b]	in absolute initial position	vino, vaso	[binɔ], [basɔ]	Eng: book

[b]	after *n*	envejecer, un vaso	[embexeθer], [umbasɔ]		
[β]	in interior position	lavar, cavar	[laβar], [kaβar]	Colloq Ger: Schwester	
	in a word, word group or breath phrase	los vinos, los vasos	[lɔzβinɔs], [lɔzβasɔs]	[ʃβɛster]	

The letter *v* is mostly pronounced [b] or [β]. The [v] sounds survives in Ladino (see Chapter 12) and is heard occasionally in Latin American speech.

w	[w]	Not really a Spanish letter. Used only in foreign names and words	wisky, Walter	[wiski], [walter]	Eng: water, west
x	[s]	in initial position	xenofobia, xerocopia	[senɔfɔβja], [serɔkopja]	
	[ks]	in interior position	taxi, examen	[taksi], [eksamen]	Eng: tax, lax
y	[j]	initial, interior, final	yo, vaya, hay	[jɔ], [baja], [aj]	Eng: yes, crayon
	[dʒ]	after *n* or *l*	inyectar, el yerno	[indʒektar], [eldʒerno]	Eng: judge, algae

One hears in Spain and in Latin America, for *yo vaya*, [dʒɔ-badʒa]. Those in Argentina and Uruguay, in the River Plate estuary, will pronounce it [ʒɔ-βaʒa], and the trend to unvoice these sounds is ever more evident, as in [ʃɔ-βaʃa]. The final *y*, however, is pronounced [j] everywhere.

z	[θ]	initial, interior, final	zarza, capaz	[θarθa], [kapaθ]	Eng: thumb, thing
	[z]	before voiced consonants	hazlo, feliz dia	[azlɔ], [felizðia]	Eng: his love, has done

In Latin America, the interdental [θ] sound has given way to a simple [s] (see Chapter 11).

Other sounds used in this book, but not generally used in Spanish:

e	[e]	closed *e* as in Italian *vedere* [vedere] or German *lebt* [lebt]
ə	[ə]	soft *e* as in English *opera* [ɔpɹə] or German *Liebe* [libə]
o	[o]	closed *o* as in Italian *dove* [dove] or German *Sohn* [zoːn]
	[ɒ]	in British *got* [gɒt]
a	[ɑ]	in German *Pause* [pɑozə]
i	[ɪ]	in English *pit* [pɪt]
u	[ʊ]	in German *Kultur* [kʊltur] or English *pool* [pʊɫ]
zh, j	[ʒ]	in *zheísmo* [ʒeismə] of the River Plate estuary of Argentina and Uruguay, *ayuda* [aʒuða]; in Ladino *hijo* [iʒɔ]
sh , x	[ʃ]	in *sheísmo* [ʃeismə] of the River Plate estuary of Argentina and Uruguay, *ayuda* [aʃuða]; in Ladino *páxaro* [paʃarɔ]
r	[ɹ]	fricative American *r* as in *red* [ɹed]
l	[ɫ]	"dark" American *l* as in *let* [ɫet]
j, g	[h]	softer sound of [x] in Latin America, as in *jota* [hɔtɑ] or *genio* [heɲɔ]
	[ç]	fricative sound of [x] in Chile, as in *gente* [çɛntɛ]

Other phonetic symbols:

	[ː]	long vowel
	[']	indicates that the **following** syllable is the stressed one, ex: [kiˈlɔmetrɔ]. This symbol was not used in this chart, but it will be used henceforth in all phonetic examples.

[a]

The New England flat *father* sound (or for that matter, *Harvard yard* can work as well) is only an approximation. Even the New England *a* can get so flat that it will not bear any resemblance to a Spanish mid-vowel [a] sound. It is best to think of a comfortable Italian [a] sound, as in the examples *casa* and *mano*. The normal British pronunciation of the words *father* and *rather* simply will not do.

[ɛ]

In this book, intended for sung Spanish, the singer will be provided with the comfortable open [ɛ] vowel, as in English *bell*, rather than with the more closed [e] sound, as in Italian *vedo*. There is very little difference in the Spanish vowel system between closed and open vowels, not even as much as in Italian. In Spanish, there are no homographs as in Italian, where identically spelled words mean different things, depending on whether the stressed vowel *e* or *o* is open or closed. For example, in Italian, *affetto* with a closed [e] means "I slice," and *affetto* with an open [ɛ] means "affection"; *corso* with a closed [o] means "a course," and *Corso* with an open [ɔ] means "Corsican." In addition, we do not wish to even suggest that singers use the tense closed [e] of German, as in *lebt* (using the same phonetic [e] symbol), which would be totally unacceptable and unidiomatic.

[i]

The English examples for this sound should really be British examples, and even then, British people tend to add off-glides to such words as *team* [təɪm]. Americans from the southern United States add on-glides and shadow vowels to this word, and instead of [tiːm], what results is [təɪəm]. It is better to imitate the Italian examples, such as *vino* and *così*.

[ɔ]

Again, the English examples *got* and *pot* should be used the British way, because in America, those words are really pronounced [gɒt] and [pɒt]. Use the Italian examples for safety. Again, we do not use the [o] symbol, because under no circumstances do we wish to suggest that singers use the German closed [o] vowel sound of *Sohn* or its cousin, the Italian [o] vowel sound of *dove*, which, though much more lax than its German counterpart, is still too closed for a true Spanish *o* sound.

[u]

Full lip rounding, as in Italian *muto*, is required for this vowel sound. The English examples are to be taken with a grain of salt, as *pool* really has an on-glide in American speech: [pəʊl].

[p] - [t] - [k]

These plosive consonants must be unaspirated. There can be no puff of air prior to the articulation, as in German or English. They must be pronounced the Italian way, as in *parto, tutto* and *quanto*.

[β] - [ð] - [ɣ]

These are the "soft," interior consonant sounds, foreign to most languages. English speakers are familiar with the [ð] of *this, them* and *those*. German speakers, in dialect, pronounce [β] in *Schwester* [ʃβɛstər]. In Spanish, we see the [ɣ] in such words as *agua*.

[θ]

This interdental consonant is easy for English speakers, as it exists in such words as *thumb, thing, thistle*. This is a strictly Castillian sound for *z* and *c* (before *e* and *i*); in Latin America, this "lisping" sound has been replaced by a simple [s] sound.

[z]

This is a rare sound in Spanish and appears only when the letter *s* assimilates with a following voiced consonant in a word group and softens to a voiced [z] sound, as in *las madres* [laz 'maðrɛs]. More about assimilation in Chapter 9.

[ɱ]

This is another case of assimilation. The letter *n* before a labiodental *f,* as in *infierno* (hell) or *infeliz* (unhappy), loses its dental articulation point and assimilates with the position of the following labiodental consonant [f], resulting in [iɱ'fiernɔ] and [iɱfe'liθ].

Now that you have an overview of Spanish sounds, let's go on to look at more specific and detailed aspects of Spanish diction for the singer.

CHAPTER 3

Vowels

Phonetic manuals for all languages go into great detail about the different shades of each vowel. Vowels can be open, closed or intermediate, depending on how one closes or opens the mouth and moves the tongue. They can be high or low, front or back, rounded or unrounded. The difference between, for example, a German closed *e* and an open *e* is a dropping of the jaw at least 6 mm, a considerable distance. Notice, too, the differing sounds of the two *a* vowels in the Spanish word *espada* (sword): the stressed *a* in the *espada* syllable is definitely more of an *a* sound than the final unstressed *a* in the *espada* syllable, which is on a shorter note. A manual of spoken Spanish will even assign a different phonetic symbol to such an unstressed *a*.

In this book, we will not concern ourselves with these minutiae. The notation of the words and the singing process will naturally homogenize all those vowels, whether they are stressed or not. Singing, by nature, has a tendency to open vowels more than speech, due to the requirements of lengthened note values, tessitura or vocal needs, such as singing vowels through or above the passaggio. This is a normal phenomenon, and the way the language is set to music by the composer will naturally supply the desired stress to the words and phrases. Therefore, in Musical Example 1, the two *a* vowels of the word *espada* will have the identical sound.

Because this book is designed for singing rather than speaking Spanish, we will dispense with much of the hair splitting about vowel qualities and provide the singer with a simple, unencumbered, singable vowel system of five vowel sounds: [i] - [ɛ] - [a] - [ɔ] - [u].

| | Fiel | es | - | pa | - | da | triun | - | fa | - | do | - | ra |
| | fjɛ | lɛs | | pa | | ða | trjum̪ | | fa | | ðɔ | | ɾa |

Musical Example 1
From "Canto a la Espada Toledana"
from zarzuela *El Huésped del Sevillano* by Jacinto Guerrero

Brevity, clarity and precision are the characteristic qualities of the Spanish vowels. It has been said that the phonetic uniformity of Spanish is greater than that of the other four languages that are predominantly spoken on the American continents (English, French, Dutch and Portuguese) and is due in great part to the simplicity and invariability of the Spanish vocalic system. (Note that in this book, the term "vocalic" is used to mean having to do with vowels. The term "vocal" will be used to refer to the voice.) There are no considerably longer or shorter vowels as in German or Italian, no weakened vowels as in Portuguese or English, and no nasalized ones as in French.

The following illustrations demonstrate how the tongue changes shape inside the mouth to form the different vowel sounds. Vowels articulated with the front (not the tip — the part immediately *behind* the tip) of the tongue raised against the hard palate are called **palatal** vowels. The highest position of the front of the tongue creates the **high front** [i] vowel, followed by the **mid high** [ɛ] vowel, with the tongue in a mid high position. Next, we have the tongue in a low position at the bottom of the mouth, creating the **low central** vowel [a]. When the tongue starts arching its back towards the soft palate or velum, the **velar** vowels are formed: first the **mid back** [ɔ], and finally, where the back of the tongue is raised to its maximum, the **high back** [u] vowel. With these two velar vowels, the lips also come into play, as they round to shape the vowel. For a complete illustration of the organs of speech, see Figure 6 on page 45.

The Palatal High Front [i]   (Written *i*, *y* or *hi*)

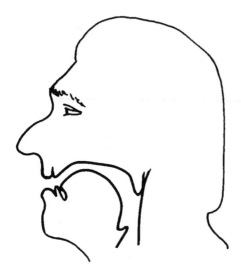

Figure 1. [i]
hijo ['ixɔ]

In producing this sound, the tip of the tongue touches the lower incisors. The front of the tongue rises against the hard palate, coming in full contact with it at both sides, and leaving in the middle a narrow passage. The lips are retracted, and the jaw is open to about 4 mm between incisors.

Speak and then sing the following examples:

[i] in initial position:

ira	['ira]	(ire)
iris	['iris]	(iris)
idiota	[i'ðjɔta]	(idiot)
imagen	[i'maxɛn]	(image)
intención	[intɛn'θjɔn]	(intention)

[i] in interior position:

milla	['miʎa]	(mile)
mira	['miɾa]	(look!)
amiga	[a'miɣa]	(friend f.)
tío	['tio]	(uncle)
higo	['iɣo]	(fig)

[i] in final position:

comí	[kɔ'mi]	(I ate)
así	[a'si]	(thus)
corrí	[kɔ'rri]	(I ran)
aquí	[a'ki]	(here)
perdí	[pɛr'ði]	(I lost)
dormí	[dɔr'mi]	(I slept)

In a diphthong (also called an on-glide or off-glide), the letter *i* is represented by the phonetic symbol [j].

[j] as off-glide:

baile	['bajlɛ]	(dance)
hay	['aj]	(there is)
peine	['pɛjnɛ]	(comb)
rey	['rɛj]	(king)
voy	['bɔj]	(I go)
sois	['sɔjs]	(you are)
cuitada	[kuj'taða]	(wretched woman)
muy	['muj]	(very)

[j] as on-glide:

labios	['laβjɔs]	(lips)
abierto	[a'βjɛrtɔ]	(open)
avion	[a'βjɔn]	(airplane)
violin	[bjɔ'lin]	(violin)
ciudad	[θju'ðað]	(city)
sabio	['saβjɔ]	(wise man)

For more about glides, see page 35. For more about the fricative glide [j], see page 88.

The Palatal Mid High [ɛ]   (Written *e* or *he*)

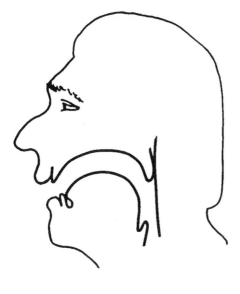

Figure 2. [ɛ]
ella [ˈɛʎa]

This mid high [ɛ] vowel is articulated with the front of the tongue raised towards the hard palate, with the mouth not quite as closed as [i]. The jaw is dropped, leaving a distance of about 8 mm between incisors. The tip of the tongue touches the lower incisors slightly less than for [i].

Speak and then sing the following examples:

[ɛ] in initial position:

ébano	['ɛβanɔ]	(ebony)
elegante	[ɛle'ɣantɛ]	(elegant)
estupido	[ɛs'tupiðʊ]	(stupid)
entiendo	[ɛn'tjɛndɔ]	(I understand)
enorme	[ɛ'nɔrmɛ]	(enormous)
hecho	['ɛtʃɔ]	(done)
hepático	[ɛ'patikɔ]	(hepatic)
hembra	['ɛmbra]	(female)

[ɛ] in interior position:

perro	['pɛrrɔ]	(dog)
guerra	['gɛrra]	(war)
puerta	['pwɛrta]	(door)
verde	['bɛrðɛ]	(green)
peine	['pɛjnɛ]	(comb)
enhebrar	[ɛnɛ'βrar]	(to thread)

[ɛ] in final position:

canté	[kan'tɛ]	(I sang)
hablé	[a'βlɛ]	(I spoke)
caminé	[kami'nɛ]	(I walked)
conquisté	[kɔŋkis'tɛ]	(I conquered)

The Palatal Low Central [a]   (Written *a* or *ha*)

Figure 3. [a]
casa ['kasa]

The low central vowel [a] requires a larger mouth opening than [i] and [ɛ]. For this low central vowel, the jaw drops, leaving about 10 mm space between incisors. The tongue is gently extended and rests in the hollow of the lower jaw, touching the lower molars. The tip of the tongue is lower than the lower incisors.

Speak and then sing the following examples:

[a] in initial position:

alma	['alma]	(soul)
arriba	[a'rriβa]	(up)
allá	[a'ʎa]	(there)
amar	[a'mar]	(to love)
arado	[a'raðɔ]	(plough)

[a] in interior position:

amado	[a'maðɔ]	(beloved)
casado	[ka'saðɔ]	(married)
cantado	[kan'taðɔ]	(sung)
estrado	[ɛs'traðɔ]	(platform)
alabado	[ala'βaðɔ]	(praised)

[a] in final position:

amada	[a'maða]	(beloved f.)
española	[ɛspa'ɲɔla]	(Spanish f.)
Alcalá	[alka'la]	(city of Alcalá)
Canadá	[kana'ða]	(Canada)
amará	[ama'ra]	(will love)

The [a] also acts as an element in rising or falling diphthongs.

[a] as an element in rising diphthongs (or on-glides):

baúl	[ba'ul]	(trunk)
Saúl	[sa'ul]	(Saul)
aún	[a'un]	(still)
laúd	[la'uð]	(lute)
Raúl	[ra'ul]	(Raoul)
caer	[ka'ɛr]	(to fall)
faraón	[fara'ɔn]	(Pharaoh)
Caín	[ka'in]	(Cain)
cuatro	['kwatrɔ]	(four)
piano	['pjanɔ]	(piano)

[a] as an element in falling diphthongs (or off-glides):

baile	['bajle]	(dance)
hay	['aj]	(there is)

The Velar Mid Back [ɔ]   (Written *o* or *ho*)

Figure 4. [ɔ]
cosa ['kɔsa]

For this sound, the jaw drops, leaving about 8 mm between the incisors. The lips round out into a relaxed oval shape. The tongue is pulled back towards the bottom of the mouth, and the back of the tongue rises toward the velum.

Speak and then sing the following examples:

[ɔ] in initial position:

orgullo	[ɔr'ɣuʎɔ]	(pride)
omitir	[ɔmi'tir]	(to omit)
ojo	['ɔxɔ]	(eye)
otro	['ɔtɾɔ]	(other)
ópera	['ɔpɛɾa]	(opera)

[ɔ] in median position:

gorro	['gɔrrɔ]	(cap)
rosa	['rɔsa]	(rose)
comer	[kɔ'mɛr]	(to eat)
golpe	['gɔlpɛ]	(a blow)
sol	['sɔl]	(sun)
cantor	[kan'tɔr]	(singer)
loco	['lɔkɔ]	(crazy)

[ɔ] in final position:

cantó	[kan'tɔ]	(he sang)
canto	['kantɔ]	(chant)
orgullo	[ɔr'ɣuʎɔ]	(pride)
caminó	[kami'nɔ]	(he walked)
camino	[ka'minɔ]	(path)

The Velar High Back [u]   (Written *u* or *hu*)

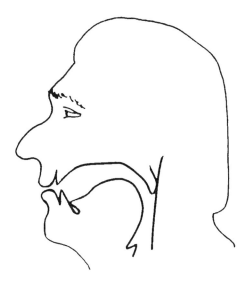

Figure 5. [u]
mucho ['mutʃɔ]

To make this sound, the lips are even more rounded than for [ɔ] and make a small oval opening. The jaw drops slightly, leaving about 4 mm distance between incisors. The tongue is pulled back towards the bottom of the mouth more than for [ɔ], and the back of the tongue rises slightly more towards the velum (soft palate).

Speak and then sing the following examples:

[u] in initial position:

uno	['unɔ]	(one)
único	['unikɔ]	(unique)
humano	[u'manɔ]	(human)
húmido	['umiðɔ]	(humid)
hulla	['uʎa]	(coal)

[u] in interior position:

mucho	['mutʃɔ]	(a lot)
gusto	['gustɔ]	(taste)
cura	['kuɾa]	(cure)
tubo	['tuβɔ]	(tube)
aceituna	[aθɛj'tuna]	(olive)
ninguno	[niŋ'gunɔ]	(no one)
rumor	[ru'mɔr]	(rumor)
capítulo	[ka'pitulɔ]	(chapter)
insulto	[in'sultɔ]	(insult)

[u] appears as the second element of falling diphthongs (or off-glides) in such words as:

sauce	['sauθɛ]	(willow)
jaula	['xaula]	(cage)
aula	['aula]	(classroom)
feudo	['fɛuðɔ]	(feud)
deuda	['dɛuða]	(debt)

u also appears as a [w] on-glide in such words as:

puerta	['pwɛrta]	(door)
tuerto	['twɛrtɔ]	(one-eyed)
cuadro	['kwaðrɔ]	(picture)
hueso	['wɛsɔ]	(bone)
agua	['aɣwa]	(water)
huésped	['wɛspɛð]	(guest)

For more about glides, see page 35.

When *u* appears in the combinations *que, qui, gue* and *gui*, the *u* is silent. For examples, see pages 92, 94 and 96.

Vowels After the Letter *h*

Since there is no [h] sound in Spanish, a word beginning with the letter *h* actually begins with the vowel sound, as in:

hacer	[a'θɛr]	(to make)
hermano	[ɛr'manɔ]	(brother)
hilo	['ilɔ]	(thread)
hombre	['ɔmbrɛ]	(man)
huérfano	['uɛrfanɔ]	(orphan)

Doubled Vowels

Notice that when vowels are doubled in a word or word group, where the last vowel of the first word or syllable is the same as the first vowel of the second word or syllable, they are pronounced as a single sound. Examples within words are:

preeminente	[prɛmi'nɛntɛ]	(preeminent)
alcoholismo	[alkɔ'lizmɔ]	(alchoholism)
vehemencia	[bɛ'mɛnθja]	(vehemence)
zoologia	[θɔlɔ'xia]	(zoology)

Some examples in word groups are:

amable encuentro	[a'maβleŋ'kwentrɔ]	(pleasant encounter)
traje estrecho	['traxɛs'tretʃɔ]	(tight suit)
cuarto oscuro	['kwartɔs'kurɔ]	(dark room)
mucho honor	['mutʃɔ'nɔr]	(much honor)
puerta abierta	['pwerta'βjerta]	(open door)
adorado hombre	[aðɔ'ra'ðɔmbrɛ]	(beloved man)
grande evento	['grandɛ'βentɔ]	(big event)

In the following musical example, notice how the double *e* vowels in the word groups *me he* and *adonde ella* are treated as a single vowel and sung on one note.

Musical Example 2

From "De este apacible rincón de Madrid"
from zarzuela *Luisa Fernanda* by F. Moreno Torroba

Two exceptions, however, are the verbs *leer* (to read) and *creer* (to believe) and their derivatives. One tends to hear among cultivated speakers an elongated [eː] vowel, thus [leːmɔs] (we read) and [kreːmɔs] (we believe).

Semivowels or Glides

Semivowels, or glides, are similar to vowels, but do not by themselves form an independent syllable. They always "lean onto" and glide into the following vowel. For example, in the word *hierro* (iron), the *i* is not syllabic, and the word is not split into three syllables, as in *hi-e-rro*. Instead, it splits into two: *hie-rro*. Therefore, the *i* is called a semivowel or glide, as it "glides" into its neighboring *e* vowel, which is the stressed element in the syllable: [jɛ]. There are eight such glides in Spanish.

Speak and then sing the following examples:

Four with the [j] glide: [ja] - [jɛ] - [jɔ] - [ju]:

ya	['ja]	(now)
yegua	['jɛɣwa]	(mare)
yo	['jɔ]	(I, myself)
diente	['djɛntɛ]	(tooth)
rabia	['rabja]	(anger)
radio	['raðjɔ]	(radio)
triunfo	[tɾi'uɱfo]	(triumph)

Four with the [w] glide: [wa] - [wɛ] - [wi] - [wɔ]:

suave	['swaβɛ]	(soft)
Sueco	['swɛkɔ]	(Swede)
Suizo	['swiθɔ]	(Swiss)
cuota	['kwɔta]	(quota)
cuatro	['kwatɾɔ]	(four)
muerte	['mwɛrtɛ]	(death)
árduo	['ardwɔ]	(arduous)

Glide syllables will usually be assigned to only one note.

Following are two musical examples of glides:

Tres per-so-nas en   u - na te   mu es - tra el   cie - lo
tɾɛs per sɔ na sɛ nu na tɛ   mwestɾael   θje lɔ

Musical Example 3

From *Seguidillas Religiosas*
by Roberto Plá

Hoy,   vie - ja,   po - bre y   fe - a
ɔj   βjɛ xa   pɔ   βɾɛi   fɛ   a

Musical Example 4

From "Vade Retro"
by Joaquín Turina

See also the section on Spanish diphthongs in the following chapter.

CHAPTER 4

Monophthongs, Diphthongs, Triphthongs and Quadraphthongs

Spanish Monophthongs vs. English Diphthongs

In English, most long vowels have a diphthong, that is, a sequence of two vowel sounds. Such words as *I, now, bacon, bone, poor, make, strike, lume* and *time* all have a diphthong in them (and in some cases with rural Southern speech, even triphthongs). Therefore, for an English speaker, the concept of a pure vowel, or monophthong — a vowel sound with no appended diphthongs, glides or "shadow vowels" — is sometimes difficult to comprehend.

Spanish contains such pure vowels or monophthongs. If a diphthong is needed, it will be so indicated by another vowel. A simple word such as *bueno* (good) should be pronounced ['bwɛnɔ], and not [bwɛjnow]. A word such as *rojo* (red) should be pronounced ['rɔxɔ], and not ['rowxow], with appended glides at the end of each syllable.

For singers, the Spanish monophthong is a great asset. It permits vocalization on pure vowels throughout the duration of the note, without having to alter the position of the speech organs. All this is advantageous to the vocal line. Because it takes extra muscular exertion to articulate the extra "shadow vowels" in [bwɛjnow], the correct Spanish pronunciation is actually much easier.

Let us compare similar-sounding (but mostly totally unrelated) words in English and Spanish. Notice how the stressed English vowel has a diphthong, whereas the Spanish has a monophthong or single vowel sound.

ENGLISH		SPANISH		
voter	['vouʊtəɹ]	vota	['bɔta]	(he votes)
motor	['moʊtəɹ]	motor	[mɔ'tɔr]	(motor)
goat	['goʊt]	gota	['gɔta]	(drop)
plain	['plɛɪn]	plena	['plɛna]	(full)
vein	['vɛɪn]	vena	['bɛna]	(vein)
mooch	['məʊtʃ]	mucho	['mutʃɔ]	(a lot)
broom	['bɹəʊm]	bruma	['bɾuma]	(fog)

Spanish Diphthongs

In Spanish, the existence of two vowels in one syllable denotes a diphthong. One of these two vowels has a stronger emphasis or a greater articulatory energy. There are rising and falling diphthongs, also called on-glide and off-glide diphthongs, respectively.

Speak and then sing the following examples:

The rising or "on-glide" diphthongs are [ja] - [jɛ] - [jɔ] and [ju].

rabia	['rabja]	(anger)
diente	['djɛntɛ]	(tooth)
labio	['laβjɔ]	(lip)
viuda	['bjuða]	(widow)

The falling or "off-glide" diphthongs are [aj] - [ɛj] - [ɔj] - [uj] - [ɛu] and [au].

baile	['bajlɛ]	(ball)
veinte	['bɛjntɛ]	(twenty)
boina	['bɔjna]	(cap)
cuidar	[kuj'ðar]	(to take care of)
feudo	['fɛuðɔ]	(feud)
jaula	['xaula]	(cage)

Spanish falling diphthongs are crisper than their English and German counterparts. In Spanish, the second element is a sharp [j] or [u], as in ['bajlɛ] or ['kausa], whereas in English, words with the similar diphthong would be phonetically transcribed as fine ['faɪn] and house ['haʊs]. In German, they would be ['faen] and ['haos].

When there are two vowels in a word which constitute different syllables, they are not treated as diphthongs, as in these examples:

continúe	con-ti-nú-e	[kɔnti'nue]	(continue)
destruír	des-tru-ír	[dɛstru'ir]	(to destroy)
dúo	du-o	['duɔ]	(duo)
paıs	pa-ís	[pa'is]	(country)
día	dí-a	['dia]	(day)
ríe	rí-e	['riɛ]	(he laughs)
tío	tí-o	['tiɔ]	(uncle)
continúa	con-ti-nú-a	[kɔnti'nua]	(continue)
reír	re-ir	[rɛ'ir]	(to laugh)
oír	o-ir	[ɔ'ir]	(to hear)
laúd	la-úd	[la'uð]	(lute)
reúno	re-ú-no	[rɛ'unɔ]	(I gather)
rodeo	ro-de-o	[rɔ'ðɛɔ]	(rodeo)
poeta	po-e-ta	[pɔ'ɛta]	(poet)
real	re-al	[rɛ'al]	(royal)
oasis	o-a-sis	[ɔ'asis]	(oasis)
faena	fa-e-na	[fa'ɛna]	(task)
ahora	a-ho-ra	[a'ɔra]	(now)

In these words, each vowel in a cluster of vowels belongs to a different syllable.

Spanish Triphthongs

A triphthong exists when there are three vowels in one syllable. As with diphthongs, there is one vowel that receives the main stress, and the others are reduced to the position of glides transcribed with [j] and [w].

Examples:

buey	['bwɛj]	(ox)
despreciais	[dɛsprɛ'θjajs]	(you despise)
averigüeis	[aβɛri'ɣwɛjs]	(you find out)
limpiais	[lim'pjajs]	(you clean)
rociais	[rɔ'θjajs]	(you water a plant)

In singing, triphthongs are usually assigned to one note.

co - mo se quie - re á u - na   ma - dre
kɔ mɔ sɛ   kjɛɾɛau na   ma   ðɾɛ

Musical Example 5
From "El Trust de los Tenorios"
by José Serrano

A mi no - vio yo le   quie - ro por - que ro - ba co - ra -
a mi   nɔβjɔ   jɔ le   kjɛɾɔ   pɔr kɛ   rɔβa   kɔ ɾa

zo - nes con su gra - cia y su sa - le - ro
θɔ nes kɔn su   ɣɾaθjaj   su sa   lɛ   ɾɔ

Musical Example 6
From "Carceleras"
from zarzuela *Las Hijas del Zebedeo* by Ruperto Chapi

Spanish Quadraphthongs: A Rare Phenomenon

A quadraphthong is a sequence of four vowels in a word group or breath phrase. These are rare and usually sung on one note.

Note the following example of a quadraphthong in de Falla's "Polo": "y quién me lo dió a entender."

me lo dió a en - ten - der ! _____

mɛ lɔ ðjɔaɛn   tɛn   dɛr

Musical Example 7

From "Polo"
by Manuel de Falla

SPANISH CONSONANTS

		PLOSIVES	NASALS	AFFRICATES	FRICATIVES	LATERALS	VIBRANTS
velar	voiced	[g]	[ŋ]		[ɣ][w]		
velar	voiceless	[k]			[x]		
palatal	voiced		[ɲ]	[dʒ]	[j]	[ʎ]	
palatal	voiceless			[tʃ]			
alveolar	voiced		[n]		[z]	[l]	[ɾ][r]
alveolar	voiceless				[s]		
dentals	voiced	[d]					
dentals	voiceless	[t]					
inter-dentals	voiced				[ð]		
inter-dentals	voiceless				[θ]		
labio-dentals	voiced		[ɱ]				
labio-dentals	voiceless				[f]		
bilabials	voiced	[b]	[m]		[β]		
bilabials	voiceless	[p]					

EXAMPLES

PLOSIVES: peso, beso, taco, dolor, caro, gato

NASALS: mano, infierno [imˈfjernɔ], nada, año [ˈaɲo], cinco [ˈθiŋkɔ]

AFFRICATES: muchacho [muˈtʃatʃɔ], conyugue [ˈkɔndʒuɣɛ]

FRICATIVES: hablar [aˈβlar], favor, cinco [ˈθiŋkɔ], adios [aˈðjɔs], salud, los mismos [lɔzˈɾiˈizmɔs],
ayuda [aˈjuða], jota [ˈxɔta], agua [ˈaɣua], afuera [aˈfwera]

LATERALS: loco, llevar [ʎɛˈβar]

VIBRANTS: amoroso [amoˈɾɔsɔ], rojo [ˈrɔxɔ]

CHAPTER 5

Spanish Consonants: Definitions

Before a discussion about consonants can begin, it's important to understand how vocal sounds are articulated.

Consonant Articulation Points

In the pronunciation of every sound, one finds an active organ, such as the lips or tongue, which, by leaning on or nearing another organ in the mouth, reduces more or less the space(s) of the exit of air at a certain position in the oral tract. The precise point in which this leaning, constriction or contact is made is called the articulation point. Each articulation point involves an active and a passive organ. Passive organs, which do not move, are the hard palate, soft palate, gums, upper lip and upper teeth. Active organs include the tongue, lower lip and jaw.

In order to facilitate the description of articulation points, we will divide the mouth cavity into various sections, from which the name of each type of articulation is taken. The tongue is one of the main organs involved in articulation, and we use the tip, the front, the blade, the middle and the back of it. We also use the lips, the gums, the gum ridge (alveoli), the hard palate (hard roof of the mouth), the soft palate or velum (soft roof of the mouth), cheeks, uvula, lower jaw (mandible) and teeth (incisors and molars).

Spanish articulation points are as follows:

BILABIAL — TWO LIPS: One lip acts against the other, the lower lip being the active organ and the upper lip being the passive one, as in [p], [b], [m] and [β]. Practice these sounds in such words as *palo* ['palɔ], *bola* ['bɔla], *mano* ['manɔ] and *hablar* [a'βlar], and feel the contact of both lips.

LABIODENTAL — LOWER LIP AND UPPER TEETH: The active organ is the lower lip, and the upper incisor teeth are the passive organs, as in [f] and [ɱ]. Practice these sounds in such words as *fuego* ['fwɛɣɔ] and *infierno* [iɱ'fiɛrnɔ], and feel the upper lip come in contact with the lower teeth.

INTERDENTAL — TONGUE BETWEEN THE TEETH: The active organ is the tip of the tongue; the passive is the edge of the upper incisor teeth, as in [θ] and [ð]. Practice the words *thumb* and *this,* then say *cinco* ['θiŋkɔ] and *adiós* [a'ðjɔs], and feel the tongue between the teeth.

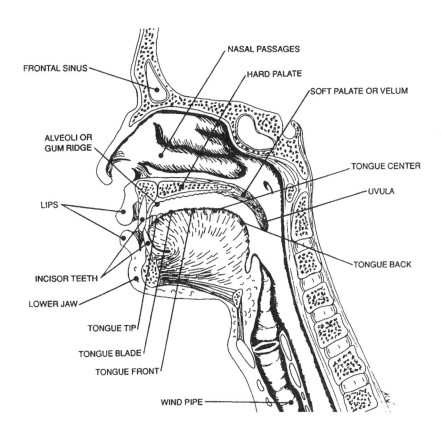

Figure 6. Organs of Speech
Points of Articulation

DENTAL — TONGUE AND INSIDE OF UPPER TEETH: The tongue tip is the active organ; the passive is the inner side of the upper incisor teeth, as in [t], [d], [n] and [l]. Practice these sounds in sequence, then in such words as *todo* ['tɔðɔ], *dados* ['daðɔs], *nada* ['naða] and *lado* ['laðɔ], and feel the tip of the tongue make contact with the upper teeth.

ALVEOLAR — TONGUE AND RIDGES OF UPPER TEETH: The tip of the tongue is the active organ, and the passive organ is the alveoli or gum ridges of the upper teeth, as in [s], [z], [ɾ], [r] and [rr]. Say these sounds in such words as *sala* ['sala], *las madres* [laz'madrɛs], *aroma* [a'ɾoma], *rojo* ['rɔxɔ] and *horror* [ɔ'rrɔr], and feel the tip of the tongue contacting (or almost contacting) the gum ridge of upper incisors.

PALATAL — TONGUE AND HARD PALATE: The active organ is the front of the tongue, and the hard palate is the passive one, as in [tʃ], [dʒ], [dj], [j], [ɲ] and [ʎ]. Say these sounds and feel the front of the tongue and hard palate meet. For [tʃ], say *champ;* for [dʒ], say *jump;* for [dj], say *adieu* in French; for [j], say *yes;* for [ɲ], say *canyon;* for [ʎ], say *figlio* in Italian.

VELAR — TONGUE AND SOFT PALATE: The active organ is the back of the tongue, and the passive is the soft palate or velum, as in [k], [g], [ŋ], [ɣ] and [x]. For [k], say *casa;* for [g], say *guante;* for [ŋ], say *bank;* for [ɣ], say *lago;* for [x], say *Bach* as in German.

For further examples of consonants grouped by articulation point, see Chapter 6.

Manner of Articulation

The mouth adjusts itself into particular positions as it prepares to pronounce each sound. Sounds are classified into the following groups based on the manner in which they are articulated:

PLOSIVES: With plosives, there is complete contact between passive and active organs. The mouth cavity stays momentarily stopped or occluded. Once the stoppage is released, the accumulated air rushes out with a little explosion, hence the term "plosive." The consonants in this category are *p, b, t, d, k* and *g,* when they represent the following sounds, respectively: [p], [b], [t], [d], [k] and [g]. Say *palo, bola, tiro, dama, caro* and *gato*. Note that in such words as *apto*, *concepto* and *adaptación*, the letter *p* is really imploded, and not exploded. In this case, it is the *t* that is the real plosive consonant.

FRICATIVES: Here there is incomplete contact between passive and active organs. The mouth cavity is constricted at some points to a narrowness through which air escapes, creating, in its friction, a sound, hence, the term fricative. The consonant sounds in this category are [f], [β], [θ], [z], [x], [ð], [l] and [ʎ], in such words as *favor* [fa′βɔr], *abuelo* [a′βuɛlɔ], *cinco* [′θiŋkɔ], *mis manos* [miz′manɔs], *jarabe* [xa′ɾaβɛ], *todo* [′tɔðɔ], *lindo* [′lindɔ] and *llave* [′ʎaβɛ].

VIBRANTS: In this case, the tip of the tongue is the active organ and produces a rapid vibrating movement against the roof of the mouth, causing minute interruptions in the escape of air. Sounds in this category are the *r* varieties. For [r], say *rio;* for [rr], say *terror;* for [ɾ], say *arado.*

AFFRICATES: A contact is made in the mouth cavity, which momentarily interrupts the escape of air, as in the case of plosives. This contact is then lightly reduced, without any sudden transition, into a constriction. The stoppage and constriction occur at the same point and between the same organs. The gradual transition from stoppage to constriction is what produces the characteristic sound in these articulations: [tʃ] and [dʒ], as in *champ* and *judge.*

NASALS: The air escapes through the nasal passages, giving a nasal resonance. For [m], say *malo;* for [n], say *nave;* for [ɲ], say *doña;* for [ŋ], say *banco;* for [ɱ], say *enfermo.*

SEMICONSONANTS (GLIDES): At the outset, the organs form a constriction. In the brief instant in which the sound is produced, the constriction relaxes and the organs form the fricative articulation towards the vowel sound. The sounds in this category are [j] and [w], as in *yes* and *water.*

Voiced and Unvoiced Consonants

It is important to know that all consonants in all languages fall into two main categories: voiced and unvoiced (in Spanish, *sonoras* and *sordas*). A voiced consonant is one that needs a vocal sound to be heard. Pronounce [b] - [d] - [g] - [v] - [z] - [l] - [β] - [n] - [m] - [ŋ] - [ɣ] - [ɲ] - [ʎ] - [ð], and you will see that nothing is heard until you activate the vocal cords — until you make a sound. A voiceless consonant is one that can be whispered and heard without the help of a vocal sound. Pronounce [p] - [t] - [k] - [ʃ] - [x] - [f] - [θ], and you will notice the difference. Voiced consonants require less articulatory effort, as they are helped by the vocal sound. Voiceless consonants, with no sound to help, need stronger articulatory effort.

Notice these voiced consonants and their unvoiced counterparts:

VOICED	UNVOICED
[b]	[p]
[d]	[t]
[g]	[k]
[ʒ]	[ʃ]
[ð]	[θ]
[v]	[f]
[ɣ]	[x]

It is important to know this distinction between voiced and unvoiced consonants, not only for this discussion of consonants, but also for the discussion about assimilation in Chapter 9.

Use of Tension or Energy

The degree of tension with which Spanish consonants are pronounced varies according to different circumstances, but principally depends on the position of the sound with relation to the stressed syllable in the word. The [θ] sound is certainly more energetic in a word like *cierto* ['θjertɔ] (certain) than in *certidumbre* [θerti'ðumbre] (certainty). In the first instance, the [θ] forms part of a stressed syllable, and in the second, it is part of an unstressed syllable in a four-syllable word. Similarly, the *s* in *jamás* [xa'mas] (never), in a stressed syllable, is pronounced with more force than the *s* in the word *lunes* ['lunes] (Monday), where it is the final consonant of the unstressed syllable.

Some Spanish consonants have two degrees of energy. For

instance, the consonants *b, d* and *g*, when in an initial position, require a strong articulation. This is particularly the case when they are in an absolute initial position (in other words, at the absolute beginning of a word or group of words, and not in the middle of a word group or breath phrase), as in *bueno* ['bwɛnɔ] (good), *dinero* [dɪ'nɛrɔ] (money), *gala* ['gala] (gala). In an interior position, the articulatory tension of the consonant will decrease somewhat, as in *lo bueno* [lɔ'βwɛnɔ] (the good), *el dinero* [ɛlðɪ'nɛrɔ] (the money), *la gala* [la'ɣala] (the gala). In the latter case, a different phonetic symbol is used to represent this softer sound.

Consonants Within a Breath Phrase

A breath phrase is a phrase that is spoken or sung in one breath. Therefore, when we refer hereafter to an "interior" consonant, we mean one that is in the middle of a word, or in the middle of a group of words in a breath phrase. The phrase *me gusta descansar de tarde* (I like to rest in the afternoon) would be spoken in one breath and transcribed thus in the IPA:

[me'ɣustaðeskan'sarðe'tarðe]

The underlined phonetic symbols coincide with the initial letters of the words *gusta, descansar* and *de*. Even though the *g* of *gusta*, the *d* of *descansar* and the *d* of *de* are initial in the word, they are considered interior in that breath phrase, and therefore softened to [ɣ] and [ð], rather than [g] and [d].

| A | to - | das las | ni - ñas | me | gus - | ta embro - | mar |
| a | tɔ | ðaz laz | ni ɲas | mɛ | ɣus | taɛmbrɔ | mar |

Musical Example 8
From "Canción contra las madamitas gorgoriteadoras"
by Antonio Rosales

For more about interior [β] - [ð] - [ɣ] sounds, see Voiced Fricatives on the following page.

Final Fricative Consonants

In the case of a final fricative consonant, such as [s], [θ] or [ð] in the words *buenos*, *feliz* and *edad,* not only does the tension lessen, but so does the exhalation of air, giving way to a lessened sound with reduced friction. Foreigners, unaware of this fact, tend to give an excessive duration and energy to the final Spanish consonants *s* [s] and *z* [θ].

The *p* [p] and *c* [k] plosives, when they appear at the end of a syllable before another plosive consonant, are usually reduced to imploded sounds, and are likewise pronounced with less force than in initial position. Examples are *doctor, concepto, aspecto, adoptar* and *tractor.* Compare with similar English words *doctor, concept, aspect, adopt* and *tractor.* Notice how in English as well, the *p* and *k* sounds are really imploded, and it is the *t* in the word that really sounds.

Voiced Plosives

When voiced plosives [b], [d] and [g] are in an absolutely initial position, the laryngeal vibrations begin, in Spanish, some six or seven hundredths of a second before the explosion. In other words, these initial voiced plosives should not be hardened as in German, but moderated as in French and Italian.

Some foreigners, especially Germans, pronounce these consonants with belated or weak vocal vibrations. These are the so-called "hard" initial voiced consonants so common in German. When they pronounce *baño* (bath), *bollo* (bun), *doma* (tames), *deja* (leaves), *gasto* (expense) or *goma* (gum), it sounds to a Spaniard as if they were saying *paño* (cloth), *pollo* (chicken), *toma* (takes), *teja* (tile), *casto* (chaste) or *coma* (comma). In order to acquire the Spanish pronunciation, which in this case resembles the Italian or French, the muscular tension must be moderated and the laryngeal vibrations clearly discernible before the explosion of the consonant.

Pronounce the following pairs of words in English and notice that the vocal cords engage a millisecond later after the unvoiced consonant (in the second word of each pair) than after the voiced consonant, which has previously engaged them:

bun — pun	goat — coat	butt — putt
dent — tent	game — came	gave — cave
back — pack	got — cot	din — tin
bet — pet	gut — cut	

Aspirated and Unaspirated Plosives

The pronunciation of *p, t* and *k* at the beginning of a syllable must be unaspirated. That is to say, no puff of air must be heard before the vowel. This "aspiration" is something that occurs commonly in English and German, where a slight *h* sound follows initial voiceless plosives, as in the German words *Keller* ['kʰɛlər], *Kultur* ['kʰʊltur], *Pause* ['pʰɑozə], *tausend* ['tʰɑozənt], or the English words *king* ['kʰɪŋ], *pit* ['pʰɪt], *tuna* ['tʰunə].

Voiced Fricatives

The voiced Spanish fricatives [β], [ð] and [ɣ] are three truly characteristic Spanish sounds that are unknown in French and Italian. In Spanish, they are used so frequently that there is rarely a phrase in which they do not occur, and in many cases, they appear several times in one word. For example: *agradecido* [aɣraðɛ'θiðɔ] (thankful), *obligación* [ɔβliɣa'θjɔn] (obligation), *avinagrado* [aβina'ɣraðɔ] (vinegary) and *comedia* [kɔ'mɛðja] (comedy). Their use in Spanish is, without doubt, much more frequent than their counterparts, the [b] - [d] - [g] plosives, which are found only in absolute initial position. The fact that they are spelled the same *(b, d, g)* must not lead us to ignore the important difference in sound, a vital matter if the Spanish language is to be pronounced correctly, in an idiomatic manner.

The Mute *h*

In correct Spanish, the *h* sound does not have the sound that it has in the English word *hat* or the German *Hut*. As in French, it existed in ancient times, but now, in words or syllables beginning with the letter *h*, the *h* is silent. The word or syllable sounds to the ear as if it begins with the vowel sound that follows, such as *hoja* ['ɔxa] (leaf), *hijo* ['ixɔ] (son), *ahoga* [a'ɔɣa] (drowns), *húmido* ['umiðɔ] (humid), *hornalla* [ɔr'naʎa] (burner), *hablar* [a'βlar] (to speak) and *hacer* [a'θɛr] (to do).

CHAPTER 6

Consonants According to Articulation Points

BILABIAL CONSONANTS [p], [b], [β], [m]

The Bilabial Plosive [p]   (Written *p*)

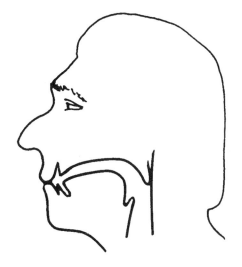

Figure 7. [p], [b]
palo ['palɔ]
bola ['bɔla]

The Spanish [p] is an unaspirated, voiceless bilabial plosive (no vocal sound is made, two lips are used, and no puff of air escapes). The lips are closed, and the tongue adopts the position of the next sound. It is the same as the Italian [p]. It resembles the English [p], except that it is unaspirated — that is, there is no puff of air escaping between the [p] and the next sound, as in the words *put* or *pond*. Practice the syllables [pi], [pɛ], [pa], [pɔ] and [pu] without aspiration.

Enunciate the [p] clearly, using the lips with energy and making sure that the vowel sound starts immediately after the parting of the lips, with no puff of air.

Speak and then sing the following examples:

[p] in initial position followed by a vowel:

pila	['pila]	(battery)
pelo	['pɛlɔ]	(hair)
pala	['pala]	(shovel)
potro	['pɔtrɔ]	(pony)
puro	['purɔ]	(pure)
pino	['pinɔ]	(pine)
peligro	[pɛ'liɣrɔ]	(danger)
paloma	[pa'lɔma]	(dove)
poco	['pɔkɔ]	(small quantity)
puño	['puɲɔ]	(fist)

[p] between vowels:

pipa	['pipa]	(pipe)
cepa	['θɛpa]	(vinestock)
papa	['papa]	(potato)
popa	['pɔpa]	(stern of a ship)
cupo	['kupɔ]	(capacity)
rápido	['rapiðɔ]	(quick)

[p] next to a consonant:

áspero	['aspɛrɔ]	(rough)
alpaca	[al'paka]	(alpaca)
empeorar	[ɛmpɛɔ'rar]	(to worsen)
pronto	['prɔntɔ]	(soon)
primo	['primɔ]	(cousin)
pleno	['plɛnɔ]	(full)
Plácido	['plaθiðɔ]	(great tenor)
espada	[ɛs'paða]	(sword)

Notice that, when followed by [t], the [p] becomes more or less implosive. While the lips are closed, the tongue readies itself to form the [t], without allowing the air to escape for the [p] explosion. Some examples are *apto, concepto, inepto* and *adopción*. Now try the English words *apt, concept, inept* and *adoption*. You will notice, as you pronounce them, that the [p] before the [t] is not really pronounced. The exact same thing happens in Spanish. It is the [t] after the [p] that is clearly heard.

When [p] is followed by *s* or *c*, it keeps its strong quality, especially in a stressed syllable, as in *eclipsar* [εklip'sar] (to eclipse), *inepcia* [i'nεpθja] (ineptitude) and *cápsula* ['kapsula] (capsule). However, when *ps* is in an initial position, the *p* is not pronounced at all. The word *psicólogo* (psychologist) is pronounced [si'kɔlɔγɔ]. In the prefix *pseudo*, the *p* is even dropped from the spelling, as in *seudónimo* [sεu'ðɔnimɔ] (pseudonym). Also, in the *pc* combination, as in *suscripción* or *transcripción*, the *p* is elided over and not pronounced at all: [suskri'θjɔn] and [transkri'θjɔn].

The Bilabial Plosive [b]   (Written *b* or *v*)

The Spanish [b] is a voiced bilabial plosive (two lips are used and it needs a vocal sound). The mouth is in the same position as for [p] (see Figure 7), but there is less muscular tension and the vocal chords vibrate, so that as you say [b], you will hear a pitch throughout the articulation of the consonant. Practice [b] on the following syllables: [bi], [bε], [ba], [bɔ] and [bu].

Speak and then sing the following examples:

[b] in initial position:

billete	[bi'ʎεtε]	(ticket)
bello	['beʎɔ]	(beautiful)
ballena	[ba'ʎena]	(whale)
bocado	[bɔ'kaðɔ]	(bit)
buho	['buɔ]	(owl)
barbero	[bar'βεrɔ]	(barber)

When *b* is in an absolute initial position and followed by a vowel, it is pronounced as a plosive [b]. Once it becomes interior, that is, in the middle of a word or a group of words in a breath phrase, it loses its plosive quality and becomes a softer [β] sound (which is really a fricative — see next section), except when preceded by [m].

[b] after the nasal [m]:

hombre	['ɔmbɾɛ]	(man)
sombra	['sɔmbɾa]	(shade)
miembro	['mjɛmbɾɔ]	(member)
embellecer	[ɛmbɛʎɛ'θɛr]	(to beautify)
cumbre	['kumbɾɛ]	(mountain top)
cambio	['kambjɔ]	(change)
timbre	['timbɾɛ]	(door bell)

Words in Spanish beginning with the letter *v* (only when it is in absolute initial position) are also pronounced with a [b] sound:

vino	['binɔ]	(wine)
vecino	[bɛ'θinɔ]	(neighbor)
vaca	['baka]	(cow)
volar	[bɔ'lar]	(to fly)
vulgar	[bul'ɣar]	(vulgar)
villano	[bi'ʎanɔ]	(villain)
venir	[bɛ'nir]	(to come)
vaso	['basɔ]	(glass)
votar	[bɔ'tar]	(to vote)
vulnerable	[bulnɛ'raβlɛ]	(vulnerable)

The Bilabial Fricative [β]   (Written *b* or *v*)

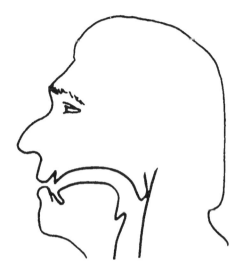

Figure 8. [β]
bobo [ˈbɔβɔ]
vivo [ˈbiβɔ]

This is the sound of the letter *b* when it is in an interior position in a word or word group in a breath phrase. It is the so-called "soft Spanish *b*." There is something like it in colloquial German, where *Schwester* [ˈʃvɛstər] and *schwach* [ˈʃvax] are pronounced as [ˈʃβɛstər] and [ˈʃβax]. The [β] does not have the plosive quality of [b]. Air escapes gently as you pronounce it, making it a fricative. All organs are poised as for [p] and [b], but the lips are slightly open and there is little muscular tension.

Speak and then sing the following examples:

libro	[ˈliβrɔ]	(book)
cabra	[ˈkaβra]	(goat)
caballo	[kaˈbaʎɔ]	(horse)
alba	[ˈalβa]	(dawn)
abajo	[aˈβaxɔ]	(below)
tubo	[ˈtuβɔ]	(tube)
pobre	[ˈpɔβrɛ]	(poor)
habitación	[aβitaˈθjɔn]	(room)

A *v* in an interior position is also pronounced as [β].

oveja	[ɔ'βɛxa]	(sheep)
avión	[a'βjɔn]	(airplane)
aventura	[aβɛn'tuɾa]	(adventure)
aviso	[a'βisɔ]	(notice)
el vaso	[ɛl'βasɔ]	(the glass)
el vino	[ɛl'βinɔ]	(the wine)
uva	['uβa]	(grape)
ovación	[ɔβa'θjɔn]	(ovation)
pino verde	[pinɔ'βɛrðɛ]	(green pine)
la verdad	[laβɛr'ðað]	(the truth)

Musical Example 9

From "Con qué la lavaré"
from *Cuatro Madrigales Amatorios* by Joaquín Rodrigo

The following example shows the letter *v* as [b] in initial position
and [β] in interior position.

Musical Example 10

From "Vos me matásteis"
from *Cuatro Madrigales Amatorios* by Joaquín Rodrigo

However, when *v* is preceded by *n* in a word or group of words, it remains [b], as in:

envejecer	[embɛxɛ'θɛr]	(to age)
un vaso	[ʊm'basɔ]	(a glass)
con valor	[komba'lɔr]	(with valor)

Notice that in the phonetic transcriptions above, the *n* is pronounced as [m] instead of [n]. This is due to assimilation of the letter *n* before the bilabial consonants *b, p* and *m*. For more about assimilation, see Chapter 9.

The Nasal Bilabial [m]   (Written *m*)

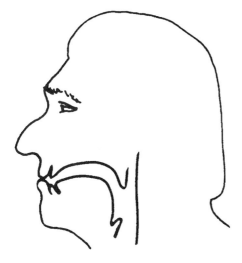

Figure 9. [m]
mano ['manɔ]

This sound requires two lips, has a vocal sound, and has a nasal resonance, making it a bilabial voiced nasal consonant. The soft palate is open, permitting the air to rise into the nasal cavities. All other organs are poised as in [p] or [b]. The pronunciation of [m] differs from [b] only in that the soft palate (velum) is open. This sound (as well as [l], [n], [ŋ] and [ɲ]) can be sustained and sung through; such sounds are called **continuants**.

Speak and then sing the following examples:

[m] before a vowel:

mira	['miɾa]	(look)
milla	['miʎa]	(mile)
mella	['meʎa]	(chink)
maravilla	[maɾa'βiʎa]	(marvel)
morena	[mɔ'ɾena]	(brunette)
música	['musika]	(music)

[m] next to a consonant:

ambición	[ambi'θjɔn]	(ambition)
hombre	['ɔmbɾe]	(man)
bomba	['bɔmba]	(bomb)
cumbre	['kumbɾe]	(apex)
empezar	[empe'θar]	(to begin)
calma	['kalma]	(calm)
asma	['azma]	(asthma)
arma	['arma]	(weapon)

[m] between vowels:

amo	['amɔ]	(master)
comer	[kɔ'mɛr]	(to eat)
cima	['θima]	(top)
amor	[a'mɔr]	(love)
rima	['rima]	(rhyme)
broma	['brɔma]	(joke)
cama	['kama]	(bed)

LABIODENTAL CONSONANTS [f], [v]

The Labiodental Fricative [f]   (Written *f*)

Figure 10. [f]
favor [fa'βɔr]

The [f] involves upper teeth and lower lip, has no vocal sound and is produced by means of air friction. It is therefore called a labiodental voiceless fricative. The lower lip softly touches the edges of the upper incisors, allowing air to escape through the lip opening. The tongue adopts the position of the following sound in the word. It is the same [f] as in English.

Speak and then sing the following examples:

[f] in initial and interior position:

finta	['finta]	(fake)
feliz	[fe'liθ]	(happy)
fama	['fama]	(fame)
foso	['fɔsɔ]	(hole)
futuro	[fu'turɔ]	(future)
ofrecer	[ɔfrɛ'θɛr]	(to offer)
huérfano	['wɛrfanɔ]	(orphan)
alfiler	[alfi'lɛr]	(pin)
enfermo	[ɛɱ'fɛrmɔ]	(sick)

The Labiodental Fricative [v]   (Written *v*)

The sound of [v], as in the English *victory,* simply does not exist in normal Spanish. A Spaniard would most probably pronounce this English word as *bictory.* The letter *v* is pronounced in Spanish as [b] or [β]. It is recognized in the spelling of words, but not in their pronunciation. Therefore, both *v* and *b* are pronounced as a bilabial plosive [b] in absolute initial position (see page 55), or as the bilabial fricative [β] in interior position or within a breath phrase (see page 57).

HISTORICAL NOTE: We find the confusion between [b] and [v] as far back as Hispano-Roman inscriptions of the first century B.C. It seems that in medieval inscriptions, the letter *b* represented the bilabial plosive [b], whereas the *v* represented the bilabial fricative [β]. Towards the beginning of the sixteenth century, this difference was abandoned, and eventually both letters were pronounced as [b] and [β]. The [v] sound survives only in the Ladino dialect of the Sephardic Jews (see Chapter 11) and in some dialectal forms of Latin American speech.

INTERDENTAL CONSONANTS [θ], [ð]

The Interdental Fricative [θ]   (Written *z* or *c*)

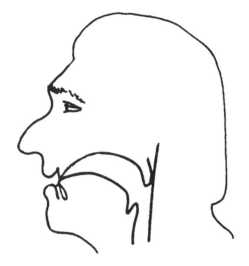

Figure 11. [θ]
cinco ['θiŋkɔ]

In Spanish, both *z* and *c* (the latter before *e* and *i)* are voiceless interdental fricatives (there is no vocal sound, and the tongue is placed between the teeth). The sound is akin to the English *th* in such words as *thumb, thimble, thin* and *throb* and is represented by the phonetic symbol [θ]. The lips are open to the shape of the vowel that follows. The tip of the tongue is placed between the edges of the upper and lower incisors, leaning gently on the uppers without stopping the escape of air. The sides of the tongue touch the inside part of the upper molars, preventing the air from escaping.

Speak and then sing the following examples:

cima	['θima]	(top)
cinco	['θiŋkɔ]	(five)
ciclo	['θiklɔ]	(cycle)
cerca	['θɛrka]	(near)
aceite	[a'θɛjtɛ]	(oil)
aceituna	[aθɛj'tuna]	(olive)

In Spanish, this "lisping" interdental sound is called *ceceo* [θɛ'θɛɔ]. It has totally disappeared from Latin American Spanish and has been replaced by a simple [s] sound (see Chapter 11 — Latin American Variants). In Latin America, a word like *cinco* (five) is simply pronounced ['siŋkɔ], and *zarza* (bramble) is pronounced ['sarsa]. The term used to describe this transformation from the lisping to the nonlisping sound is *seseo* [sɛ'sɛɔ]. For singers performing Castillian music from Spain, *ceceo* is advisable; for Latin American music, *seseo* is recommended. Although a native Spanish singer might choose to sing Latin American songs in his accustomed *ceceo* fashion, a non-native singer is urged to use the simpler *seseo* to avoid sounding affected.

> **HISTORICAL NOTE:** It is interesting to note that the lisping sound of the Castillian *c* (before *e* and *i*) and *z* is not, as many claim, an affectation that began in olden days because of the lisping of some Spanish king (probably Phillip II, a Hapsburg monarch whose pronounced underbite could have given him trouble with sibilant consonants), for whom the entire population, out of respect, or perhaps, believing this to be "high court" speech, imitated their sovereign's speech defect. Although it makes for good linguistic fiction, this is not the case at all.
>
> The lisping sound of *c* as in *Cecilia* [θɛ'θilja] or *z* in *zaragoza* [θara'ɣɔθa] arose for purely phonetic reasons. It sprang from the fact that in old Spanish, there were two affricate sounds (an affricate sound is one that is a combination of a plosive and a fricative in quick succession), the [ts] and the [dz], one a voiceless affricate (as in English *puts*) and the other a voiced affricate (as in English *adze*). However, the affricate sounds of [ts] and [dz] did not sit well in the Spanish mouth, which found difficulty articulating this most un-Spanish combination of sounds. By the sixteenth century, the old form gave way to a more forward articulation, becoming the fricative sounds of today. For awhile, it even maintained a voiced and unvoiced sound, finally emerging as one voiceless interdental fricative, the [θ].

The Interdental Fricative [ð]   (Written *d*)

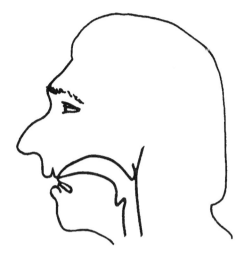

Figure 12. [ð]
adios [a'ðjɔs]

In the voiced interdental fricative [ð] (a vocal sound with the tongue between the teeth, involving friction of air), the tip of the tongue lightly touches the edges of the upper incisors, without stopping the air flow completely. Muscular tension is weak for this "soft *d*," which is akin to the English *th* in such words as *this* and *that*. The fricative [ð] is used whenever the letter *d* is not absolutely initial, that is, when it is in the middle of a word or a breath phrase, or when it comes after *n* or *l*.

Speak and then sing the following examples:

[ð] in interior position:

cocido	[kɔ'θiðɔ]	(boiled)
dormido	[dɔr'miðɔ]	(asleep)
dedo	['deðɔ]	(finger)
hablado	[a'βlaðɔ]	(spoken)
mudo	['muðɔ]	(mute)
tu dinero	[tuði'nɛɾɔ]	(your money)
los dolores	[lɔzðɔ'lɔɾɛs]	(the pains)
es duro	[ɛz'ðuɾɔ]	(is hard)
madre	['maðɾɛ]	(mother)

When the letter *d* [ð] is in final position, it acquires an even softer texture, with more of a fricative quality, as in the following words:

[ð] in final position:

Madrid	[ma'ðɾið]	(Madrid)
bebed	[bɛ'βɛð]	(drink it)
verdad	[bɛr'ðað]	(truth)
usted	[us'tɛð]	(you)
sed	['sɛð]	(thirst)

Musical Example 11 shows the use of both initial [d] (see page 70) and interior [ð] in one phrase. The initial syllable *de* begins with [d], while the initial *d* in *donde* becomes [ð], because it is in interior position in a word group. The *de* syllable in *donde* is again [d], because it is preceded by a nasal *n*.

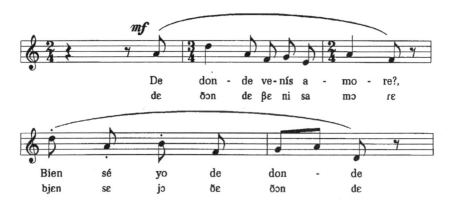

Musical Example 11
From "De donde venís amore"
from *Cuatro Madrigales Amatorios* by Joaquín Rodrigo

In the participle forms of *"ado,"* as in *pintado* (painted), *cantado* (sung), *hablado* (spoken) and *trabajado* (worked), *"ado"* tends sometimes, in "Gypsy Spanish" or popular speech, to be almost reduced to an [aɔ] diphthong, resulting in the popular pronunciations *cantao, pintao, hablao* and *trabajao*. The reason we mention this phenomenon of "popular speech" is that sometimes in songs or zarzuela arias, this pronunciation is required, as in Valverde's "Clavelitos" (Musical Example 12). Here, the spelling in the phrases *con los ojos cerraos* and *rojos y pintaos* is changed from the correct spelling *cerrados* and *pintados*.

Musical Example 12
From "Clavelitos"
by Antonio Valverde

In many zarzuela songs, the popular or "Gypsy" pronunciation is desired. In most cases the composer will provide the spelling of the popular pronunciation by simply misspelling the words, using, for example, *usté* for *usted* and *Madri* for *Madrid* (Musical Example 13), *pa* for *para* (Musical Example 14), *tóo* for *todo* and *sentío* for *sentido* (Musical Example 15).

Musical Example 13
From "Ay Madrileña"
from *La Chulapona* by F. Moreno Torroba

Musical Example 14
From "Romanza de Sagrario"
from zarzuela *La Rosa del Azafrán* by Jacinto Guerrero

Musical Example 15
From "Guajiras"
from zarzuela *La Revoltosa* by Ruperto Chapi

DENTAL CONSONANTS [t], [d]

The Dental Plosive [t]   (Written *t*)

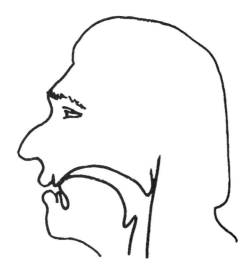

Figure 13. [t], [d]
tarde ['tarðɛ]
dama ['dama]

The Spanish [t] is a voiceless dental unaspirated plosive (that is, produced with no vocal sound, the tongue resting against the upper teeth, with no puff of air escaping, and formed by an explosion of air). The lips are open to the position of the vowel that follows, with the tip of the tongue resting on the inside face of the upper incisors, causing a complete stoppage of air.

The main difference between the Spanish [t] and the German or English sound is that the Spanish consonant, like its sister, the Italian [t], is unaspirated. There is no puff of air before the utterance of the [t] sound, which is accomplished by pressing the tip of the tongue strongly against the inside of the upper teeth. Try putting the tip of the tongue weakly against the upper teeth, and you will notice the puff of air escaping before the utterance of the [t] sound. This is called aspiration, and it is strictly for German and English. Practice [ti] - [tɛ] - [ta] - [tɔ] - [tu] using no aspiration.

Speak and then sing the following examples:

[t] in initial position:

tiro	['tiɾɔ]	(shot)
temor	[tɛ'mɔr]	(fear)
tapa	['tapa]	(lid)
toldo	['tɔlðɔ]	(awning)
túnica	['tunika]	(tunic)

[t] between vowels:

cita	['θita]	(date)
bata	['bata]	(apron)
bonita	[bɔ'nita]	(pretty)
bota	['bɔta]	(boot)
rata	['rata]	(rat)

[t] next to a consonant:

tripa	['tɾipa]	(tripe)
tres	['tɾɛs]	(three)
trampa	['tɾampa]	(trap)
tronco	['tɾɔŋkɔ]	(tree trunk)
trucha	['tɾutʃa]	(trout)
espanto	[ɛs'pantɔ]	(fright)
trabajo	[tɾa'βaxɔ]	(work)
alto	['altɔ]	(tall)

The Dental Plosive [d]   (Written *d*)

The Spanish [d] is a voiced dental plosive (that is, it has a vocal sound, the tip of the tongue rests against the inside of the upper incisors, and it is formed by a weak explosion of air). All organs of the mouth are in the same position as for [t] (see Figure 13), except that the muscular tension is reduced and the vocal cords are active, giving the consonant its voiced quality. In Spanish, the letter *d* is pronounced [d], rather than [ð], when it is in absolute initial position or when it comes after *n* or *l.*

Speak and then sing the following examples:

[d] in initial position:

dibujo	[di'βuxɔ]	(drawing)
deseo	[de'sɛɔ]	(desire)
dados	['daðɔs]	(dice)
dolor	[dɔ'lɔr]	(pain)
drama	['drama]	(drama)
duda	['duða]	(doubt)

[d] after *n:*

lindo	['lindɔ]	(pretty)
blando	['blandɔ]	(soft)
mundo	['mundɔ]	(world)
hondo	['ɔndɔ]	(deep)
vender	[βɛn'dɛr]	(to sell)

[d] after *l:*

tilde	['tildɛ]	(tilde [~])
rebelde	[rɛ'βɛldɛ]	(rebel)
balde	['baldɛ]	(bucket)
toldo	['tɔldɔ]	(awning)
humilde	[u'mildɛ]	(humble)

It is important to note that there is a marked tendency among Americans to reduce the intervocalic (between vowels) *d* to a flipped [ɾ] sound. It is what I call the "spaghetti *d*," from the fact that the well-loved pasta, pronounced crisply as [spa'gettːi] in Italian, is pronounced [spə'gɛɾi] in America. The crisp *tt* is reduced to a mere flipped [ɾ]. The same occurs whenever an American (or Briton, for that matter), finds a *d* between vowels: It gets reduced to an [ɾ] flip or "spaghetti *d*." Consider such "slangy" American words as *today* [tə'ɾeɪ], *two dollars* [tu'ɾɔɫəs], *bedding* ['bɛɾɪŋ], *modal* ['mouɾəɫ], *model* ['mɔɾəɫ] and *idyll* ['aɪɾɫ].

Practice saying and singing the following Spanish words, making sure that you use a [d] in the left column and an [ɾ] flip in the right one. As you can see, incorrect pronunciation will make quite a difference in the meaning of the words.

todo	['toðo]	(everything)	toro	['toɾo]	(bull)
cada	['kaða]	(every)	cara	['kaɾa]	(face)
pida	['piða]	(ask for)	pira	['piɾa]	(pyre)
modo	['moðo]	(a way)	Moro	['moɾo]	(a Moor)
mida	['miða]	(measure)	mira	['miɾa]	(look!)
cantada	[kan'taða]	(sung)	cantara	[kan'taɾa]	(if she sang)
amada	[a'maða]	(beloved)	amara	[a'maɾa]	(if he loved)
pudo	['puðo]	(he could)	puro	['puɾo]	(cigar)
codo	['koðo]	(elbow)	coro	['koɾo]	(chorus)

ALVEOLAR CONSONANTS [s], [z], [n], [l], [ɾ], [r], [rr]

The Predorsal Alveolar [s]   (Written *s*)

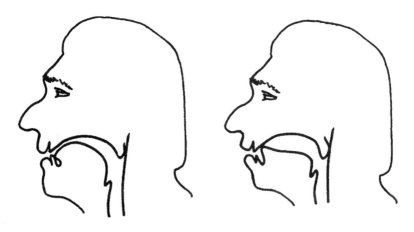

Spanish Predorsal *s*   **Italian Alveolar *s***

Figure 14. [s]
sala ['sala]

The Spanish [s] is a voiceless alveolar fricative (that is, it has no vocal sound, the tongue comes in contact with the upper gum ridges or alveoli, and it is produced by friction of escaping air). It is also called "predorsal," because its sibilant sound is not as sharp as its cousin's, the Italian [s] of *salute* and *soave*. It is made by the front end of the tongue (predorsum) making contact with the alveoli, rather than the tip of the tongue (Figure 14). One could say that the Spanish predorsal *s* sounds a bit like the Texas pronunciation of, *Say, I said something serious at the seminar on Saturday*, with the *s* palatalized to almost sound like, *Shay, I shaid shomething sherious at the sheminar on Shaturday* — pretty much using the *s* of former President Lyndon Johnson. It's definitely something that has to be heard to be imitated. The true Castillian [s] has that semipalatal, predorsal sound. The tongue edges lean against the gums at both sides of the mouth and against the upper molars.

Speak and then sing the following examples:

[s] in initial position:

silla	['siʎa]	(chair)
seda	['seða]	(silk)
sala	['sala]	(living room)
solo	['sɔlɔ]	(alone)
sucio	['suθjɔ]	(dirty)

[s] in interior position:

casa	['kasa]	(house)
cosa	['kɔsa]	(thing)
misa	['misa]	(Mass)
uso	['usɔ]	(use)
mesa	['mɛsa]	(table)

[s] next to a consonant:

listo	['listɔ]	(ready)
esto	['ɛstɔ]	(this)
basta	['basta]	(enough!)
postal	[pɔs'tal]	(postcard)
busto	['bustɔ]	(bosom)
insolente	[insɔ'lɛntɛ]	(insolent)

In many regions of Italy, one also hears that predorsal [s]. In Latin American Spanish, however, it has totally disappeared, except in a few pockets of population in the Andes and other locations (see Chapter 11— Latin American Variants).

The Alveolar "Voiced *s*" [z]   (Written *s*)

Spanish people don't feel comfortable with the [z] sound, as in English *zebra*. It occurs in Spanish only when the letter *s* precedes a voiced consonant (a consonant that engages vocal chord activity, such as *m, n, l, b, d, g)* or through assimilation (see Chapter 9). It then loses its voiceless sibilant quality and becomes a voiced [z]. For instance, the word *muslo* (thigh) is pronounced ['muzlɔ], and not ['muslɔ]. Due to the fact that the letter *l*, which follows the letter *s*, is voiced, the consonant cluster *sl* becomes totally voiced. The same will occur in the word group *los mismos* (the same). It is pronounced [lɔz'mizmɔs] for the same reason: the letter *m*, being voiced, causes the *s* that precedes it to assimilate and become a voiced [z] rather than a voiceless [s].

It is very important not to confuse the [z] sound with the letter *z*. The letter *z*, as we have seen above under Interdental Consonants (see page 63), is a [θ] sound.

Speak and then sing the following examples:

mismo	['mizmɔ]	(same)
mis labios	[miz'laβjɔs]	(my lips)
mes de Mayo	['mezðe'majɔ]	(month of May)
mesmerizado	[mɛzmɛɾi'θaðɔ]	(mesmerized)
más malo	['maz'malɔ]	(worse)
los maté	[lɔzma'tɛ]	(I killed them)
asno	['aznɔ]	(donkey)
esbelto	[ɛz'βɛltɔ]	(svelte)
isla	['izla]	(island)
tus besos	[tuz'βɛsɔs]	(your kisses)
los nenes	[lɔz'nɛnɛs]	(the babies)

Notice that in all of these examples, the *s* precedes a voiced consonant. Compare with the similar phenomenon in Italian, when *s* precedes a voiced consonant and becomes a [z] sound in such words as *sdegno* ['zdeɲɲo], *smanie* ['zmanjɛ], *sbaglio* ['zbaʎʎɔ], *snello* ['znɛl:lɔ], *svago* ['zvagɔ] and *sgombra* ['zgombra].

Romance languages prefer to have synchronic consonant clusters with the letter *s* — that is, either all voiced or all unvoiced. It is hard for an Italian to say *small slice* or *slow slide*. He will probably say *zmall zlice* and *zlow zlide*. Spanish speakers, unaccustomed as they are to starting any word with an *s* followed by a consonant, would most likely pronounce the above as *ezmall ezlice* and *ezlow ezlide*. It is also interesting to note that a Hispanic or Spanish speaker is definitely uncomfortable with the [z] sound. Even erudite and cultured Spanish speakers will pronounce the word *civilization* as [siβili'sɛjʃon] (with the *v* most probably becoming a [β] as well). The word *amazing* will probably become [a'mejsiŋ], and so on.

In the American Southwest, especially New Mexico, where there is a marked Hispanic linguistic influence, I have noticed that such words as *shoes, cows, goes, toes, yours,* all of which have a [z] sound at the end, are often pronounced ['ʃus] - ['kaʊs] - ['goʊs] - ['toʊs] - ['jʊrs], all with an [s] sound at the end. The [z] at the end of those words is probably not too comfortable for these Spanish-influenced speakers of the English language.

The Alveolar Nasal [n]   (Written *n*)

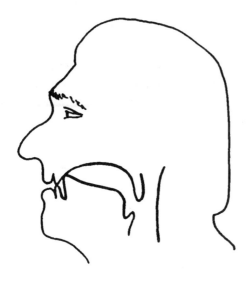

Figure 15. [n]
nada ['naða]

The [n] is a voiced alveolar nasal (it has a vocal sound, the tip of the tongue touches the alveoli or ridge of the upper teeth, and it resonates in the nasal cavities). The lips and jaws are poised for the sound that follows. The tip of the tongue meets the alveoli, while the side edges of the tongue touch the gums and molars, creating a total occlusion of the mouth. The soft palate is open, and the exhaled air exits through the nose.

Speak and then sing the following examples:

[n] in initial position followed by a vowel:

niño	['niɲɔ]	(boy)
nene	['nɛnɛ]	(baby)
necio	['nɛθjɔ]	(oafish)
nada	['naða]	(nothing)
nadie	['naðjɛ]	(no one)
noche	['nɔtʃɛ]	(night)
noticia	[nɔ'tiθja]	(news)
nunca	['nuŋka]	(never)
nube	['nuβɛ]	(cloud)

[n] next to a consonant:

finta	['finta]	(fake)
tinta	['tinta]	(ink)
tentar	[tɛn'tar]	(to try)
inventar	[imbɛn'tar]	(invent)
manto	['mantɔ]	(mantle)
cantar	[kan'tar]	(to sing)
montar	[mɔn'tar]	(to mount)
punto	['puntɔ]	(dot, spot, period)
difunto	[di'funtɔ]	(deceased)
ensayar	[ɛnsa'jar]	(to rehearse)
ensuciar	[ɛnsu'θjar]	(to soil)
entristecer	[ɛntɾistɛ'θɛr]	(to sadden)
enterrar	[ɛntɛ'rrar]	(to bury)
el novio	[ɛl'nɔβjɔ]	(the bridegroom)

[n] in final position:

cantan	['kantan]	(they sing)
piden	['piðɛn]	(they ask for)
beben	['bɛβɛn]	(they drink)
sartén	[sar'tɛn]	(frying pan)
Copán	[kɔ'pan]	(city in Mexico)
charlatán	[tʃarla'tan]	(charlatan)
caimán	[kaj'man]	(type of crocodile)
Petén	[pɛ'tɛn]	(region in Central America)
hablarán	[aβla'ran]	(they will speak)
limón	[li'mɔn]	(lemon)
atún	[a'tun]	(tuna)

To see how the [n] changes articulation point according to which consonant follows, see Chapter 9 — Assimilation. Also, see how the final [n] becomes velarized to an [ŋ] sound in parts of Latin America in Chapter 11 — Latin American Variants.

The Alveolar [l]   (Written *l*)

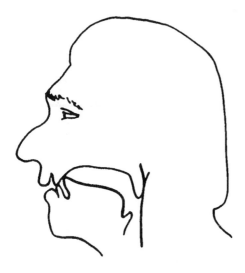

Figure 16. [l]
lobo [ˈloβɔ]

    The Spanish [l] is a voiced alveolar lateral consonant (the tip of the tongue comes in contact with the alveoli or gums of the upper incisors, it involves vocal chord activity, and air escapes from an opening at the side of the mouth). At each side of the mouth (or one side only, depending on the speaker), there remains between the tongue and molars an elongated opening through which air escapes, producing a soft friction. The top of the tongue is almost straight, and it never assumes the raised velar (soft palate) position of the American *l*, which must be avoided in Spanish (although it is used in Portuguese, Catalan and Russian). It is the same [l] that is used in Italian.

Speak and then sing the following examples:

[l] in initial position followed by a vowel:

linda	['linda]	(beautiful f.)
lima	['lima]	(file)
lema	['lɛma]	(motto)
legar	[lɛ'ɣar]	(leave in a will)
lado	['laðɔ]	(side)
lata	['lata]	(tin)
lodo	['lɔðɔ]	(mud)
lobo	['lɔβɔ]	(wolf)
lupa	['lupa]	(magnifying glass)
lumbre	['lumbrɛ]	(fire, light)

[l] next to a consonant:

filtro	['filtrɔ]	(filter)
tilde	['tildɛ]	(tilde [~])
balde	['baldɛ]	(bucket)
endeble	[ɛn'dɛβlɛ]	(feeble)
hablar	[a'βlar]	(to speak)
alpargata	[alpar'gata]	(sandal)
altero	[al'tɛrɔ]	(haughty)
enlodar	[ɛnlɔ'ðar]	(to muddy)
muslo	['muzlɔ]	(thigh)
perla	['pɛrla]	(pearl)

[l] in final position:

mil	['mil]	(thousand)
candil	[kan'dil]	(candle)
miel	['mjɛl]	(honey)
fiel	['fjɛl]	(faithful)
mal	['mal]	(bad, badly)
fatal	[fa'tal]	(fatal)
sol	['sɔl]	(sun)
árbol	['arβɔl]	(tree)
azul	[a'θul]	(blue)
Raúl	[ra'ul]	(Raul)

The Alveolar Flipped [ɾ]   (Written *r*)

Figure 17. [ɾ]
aro ['aɾɔ]

    The Spanish flipped [ɾ] is a single voiced alveolar vibrant (it has a vocal sound, the tip of the tongue is against the alveoli or gum ridge, and it taps once). The lips and jaws are set according to the sound that follows. The sides of the tongue lean against the inside and gums of the upper molars and close off the air at both sides of the palate. The tip of the tongue rises with great speed, touches the edges of the upper incisors, and then quickly returns to the articulatory position of the sound that follows.

    It is absolutely imperative that the tongue accomplish a single tap only, otherwise a multiple "rolled" sound will occur, creating the quite different [r] sound, which is discussed below. The flipped [ɾ] is found in Spanish in intervocalic positions (between vowels), either within one word or a group of words, and when preceded by a consonant other than *l, n* or *s*. When preceded by *l, n* or *s*, it becomes a rolled [r] sound.

Speak and sing the following examples:

[ɾ] in interior position:

iris	['iɾis]	(iris)
pera	['pɛɾa]	(pear)
muera	['mwɛɾa]	(may he die)
cara	['kaɾa]	(face)
parada	[pa'ɾaða]	(bus stop)
coro	['kɔɾɔ]	(chorus)
Moro	['mɔɾɔ]	(a Moor)
muro	['muɾɔ]	(wall)
puro	['puɾɔ]	(pure, cigar)
amar así	[amaɾa'si]	(to love like that)
comer asado	[kɔmɛɾa'saðɔ]	(to eat barbecue)
pedir agua	[pɛði'ɾaɣwa]	(to ask for water)
por eso	[pɔ'ɾɛsɔ]	(for that reason)
por allá	[pɔɾa'ʎa]	(over there)
ser así	[sɛɾa'si]	(to be like this)

[ɾ] preceded by consonants other than *l*, *n* and *s*:

tribu	['tɾiβu]	(tribe)
triunfo	[tɾi'uɱfɔ]	(triumph)
breve	['bɾɛβɛ]	(brief)
creer	[kɾɛː'ɛr]	(to believe)
agravio	[a'ɣɾaβjɔ]	(insult)
grano	['gɾanɔ]	(grain)
atroz	[a'tɾɔθ]	(atrocious)
trucha	['tɾutʃa]	(trout)
brusco	['bɾuskɔ]	(brusque)
fresco	['fɾɛskɔ]	(fresh)
frasco	['fɾaskɔ]	(flask)
frígido	['fɾixiðɔ]	(frigid)
drama	['dɾama]	(drama)

The Alveolar Rolled [r] and [rr]   (Written *r* or *rr*)

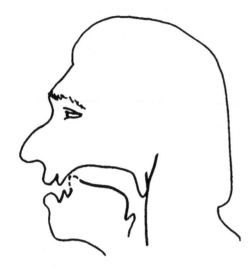

Figure 18. [r], [rr]

rojo ['rɔxɔ]

carro ['karrɔ]

The Spanish [r] is a voiced multiple alveolar vibrant (it has a vocal sound, the tongue tip is against alveoli or gum ridges, and it flaps rapidly to make a "rolling" sound). The lips and jaw are set for the sound that follows. The sides of the tongue are set as for [ɾ] and close off the escape of air. The tip of the tongue curves upward until it touches the highest part of the upper alveoli. The body of the tongue retracts towards the bottom of the mouth, and its front part adopts a concave shape. At the same time as its tip touches the alveoli, it is pushed away by a current of expelled air. The tongue's own elasticity makes it return to the initial point of contact, but again it is pushed outward with great strength. This sequence of movements is repeated many times, creating the rolling effect of the trilled [r]. The [rr] is the same sound, but with a bit more energy.

At each contact with the alveoli, the air escape is momentarily interrupted, resulting in a rapid series of little explosions. This is the sound we need in Spanish when *r* is initial, when it is preceded by *l*, *n* or *s*, and when it is doubled, as in *carro*. It is important to notice that in Spanish, contrary to Italian, all initial *r*'s must be rolled, even within a breath phrase. (In Italian, we have the option of sometimes flipping these initial *r*'s.)

Speak and then sing the following examples:

[r] in initial position:

río	['riɔ]	(river)
rival	[ri'val]	(rival)
reflejo	[re'flexɔ]	(reflection)
remar	[rɛ'mar]	(to row)
rama	['rama]	(a branch)
rápido	['rapiðɔ]	(swift)
rojo	['rɔxɔ]	(red)
robusto	[rɔ'βustɔ]	(robust)
rumor	[ru'mɔr]	(rumor)
ruína	[ru'ina]	(ruin)

[r] preceded by consonants *l*, *n* and *s:*

honrado	[ɔn'raðɔ]	(honest)
enredo	[ɛn'reðɔ]	(an entanglement)
Henrique	[ɛn'rikɛ]	(Henry)
el ruinoso	[ɛlrui'nɔsɔ]	(the ruinous)
mas rápido	[maz'rapiðɔ]	(quicker)
es rojo	[ez'rɔxɔ]	(it is red)
Israel	[izra'ɛl]	(Israel)
alrededor	[alrɛðɛ'ðɔr]	(around)
el remedio	[ɛlrɛ'mɛðjɔ]	(the medicine)
del ramo	[dɛl'ramɔ]	(of the branch)

[r] before a consonant:

firma	['firma]	(signature)
enfermo	[ɛm'fermɔ]	(sick)
arte	['artɛ]	(art)
arder	[ar'ðɛr]	(to burn)
orden	['ɔrðɛn]	(order)
portero	[pɔr'tɛrɔ]	(doorman)
hurto	['urtɔ]	(theft)
marsupial	[marsu'pjal]	(marsupial)
perla	['pɛrla]	(pearl)

[rr] in words containing a double *rr:*

mirra	['mirra]	(myrrh)
perro	['pɛrrɔ]	(dog)
hierro	['jɛrrɔ]	(iron)
amarrar	[ama'rrar]	(to tie up)
arrasar	[arra'sar]	(to raze)
corroer	[kɔrrɔ'er]	(to corrode)
horror	[ɔ'rrɔr]	(horror)
terror	[te'rrɔr]	(terror)
arruinar	[arrui'nar]	(to ruin)

In final position, the *r* should be gently pronounced as a sound between the flipped [ɾ] and rolled [r], but not too rolled.

[ɾ] in final position:

amar	[a'mar]	(to love)
comer	[kɔ'mer]	(to eat)
matar	[ma'tar]	(to kill)
huir	[u'ir]	(to flee)
morder	[mɔr'ðer]	(to bite)
ser	['ser]	(to be)
cantar	[kan'tar]	(to sing)
perder	[per'ðer]	(to lose)

Note that the pronunciation of the following words — whether with flipped [ɾ] or rolled [r] — changes their meaning. Pronounce the first column with a flip and the second with a roll:

pero	['pɛrɔ]	(but)	perro	['pɛrrɔ]	(dog)
cero	['θɛrɔ]	(zero)	cerro	['θɛrrɔ]	(hill)
coro	['kɔrɔ]	(chorus)	corro	['kɔrrɔ]	(I run)
caro	['karɔ]	(expensive)	carro	['karrɔ]	(car)
ahora	[a'ɔra]	(now)	ahorra	[a'ɔrra]	(he saves)
para	['para]	(for)	parra	['parra]	(vine plant)
careta	[ka'rɛta]	(facing)	carreta	[ka'rrɛta]	(cart)

Practicing Rolled and Flipped *r*'s

The rolled and flipped *r* sounds do not come easily to speakers of American English. The *r* that we use in American speech is really a fricative [ɹ] sound and involves the lips to a great extent. The rolled [r] or flipped [ɾ] are truly not American speech sounds. The British use it, of course, and we hear it often in cultivated British speech, especially when spoken by great actors such as Olivier, Gielgud, Guinness or Richardson. In Spanish, we need to learn to roll and flip the *r*. This will take some practice.

In England, one will undoubtedly hear a phrase like *very merry* with such flipped *r* sounds. Let us now change the *r* for a *d* sound and say *veddy meddy*. If you pronounce *veddy meddy* in a quick fashion over and over, you will probably find that the tongue, after a few times, "trips" into a flipped [ɾ], which is what is needed in Spanish.

The [d] is definitely the best starting point for learning the flipped [ɾ], and if one can imitate the British as they pronounce such words as *merit, spirit, Caroline, starry, fury, horrid* and *fiery*, one is on the way. Substitute a *d* for all *r*'s in the above words and say *medit, spidit, Cadoline, stady, fudy, hodid* and *fiedy*, and you will soon find yourself flipping those *r*'s in British fashion.

Practice by saying a syllable with *d*, thus: [daaadaaadaaa], [deeedeeedeee], [diiidiiidiii], etc. on all vowels. Then change the second and third consonant to [ɾ], thus: [daaaɾaaaɾaaa]. [deeeɾeeeɾeee], [diiiɾiiiɾiii], etc. Eventually change all *d*'s to [ɾ], thus: [ɾaaaɾaaaɾaaa], [ɾeeeɾeeeɾeee], [ɾiiiɾiiiɾiii], etc.

When you feel that the flipped [ɾ] is working, then try to prolong it into a rolled [r], which is nothing more than an extended series of flips. Keep practicing until the tip of the tongue responds and you can roll an [r]. Do not overdo these exercises. Give the tongue time to relax.

Some singers learn to roll the *r* by allowing their breath to activate the tip of the tongue until it vibrates, for it is the breath that causes the tip of the tongue to trill against the teeth. Place the tip of the tongue toward the top of the upper teeth, as if to pronounce a *d*, but without actually making contact with the teeth, so as to give the tongue room to trill. Then expel your breath suddenly with a forceful puff. If done correctly, the tongue will vibrate and produce an [r]. If you succeed in getting some kind of lingual trill, even two or three, keep practicing at short intervals until a prolonged roll is obtained. Remember to relax your jaw and tongue.

PALATAL CONSONANTS [tʃ], [dʒ], [j], [ɲ], [ʎ]

The Palatal Affricate [tʃ]   (Written *ch*)

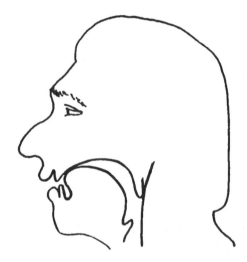

Figure 19. [tʃ]
chico ['tʃikɔ]

This is an affricate palatal voiceless consonant (no vocal sound, palate is involved). An affricate is a combination of a plosive consonant followed quickly by a fricative one. In this case the plosive element is [t] and the fricative element is [ʃ]. Pronounced together, they form the sound of *ch* in such English words as *champ, chimney* and *chimpanzee.* The lips are in the position of the vowel that follows. The tongue rises in a convex manner, touching a large area of the hard palate on each side of the mouth. The front of the tongue continues to touch the front of the palate and alveoli, interrupting the flow of air for a moment.

Speak and then sing the following examples:

China	['tʃina]	(China)
chico	['tʃiko]	(little)
hechizo	[e'tʃiθo]	(bewitchment)
écheme	['etʃeme]	(throw me out)
chapa	['tʃapa]	(tin foil)
cacharra	[ka'tʃarra]	(jalopy)
chorro	['tʃorro]	(stream of water)
cachorro	[ka'tʃorro]	(puppy)
chupar	[tʃu'par]	(to suck)
corcho	['kortʃo]	(cork)
mucho	['mutʃo]	(a lot)
muchacho	[mu'tʃatʃo]	(young boy)
chiquita	[tʃi'kita]	(little one f.)

The Palatal Affricate [dʒ]   (Written y)

Figure 20. [dʒ]
yugo ['dʒuɣɔ]

This is another affricate, but voiced, since its two elements are a voiced [d] and a voiced [ʒ]. It requires the exact same articulation as the [tʃ] affricate, but with less muscular tension, because of the fact that it is voiced and has a vocal sound to help it be heard. It is used in the English words *judge, jump* and *jam.* The [dʒ] sound is written *y,* preceded by *n* or *l.*

Speak and then sing the following examples:

cónyugue	['kɔndʒuɣɛ]	(bridegroom)
inyectar	[indʒɛk'tar]	(to inject)
el yunque	[ɛl'dʒuŋkɛ]	(the anvil)
enyesar	[ɛndʒe'sar]	(put in a cast)
el yerno	[ɛl'dʒɛrnɔ]	(the brother-in-law)

The Fricative Glide [j]   (Written *y* or *hi*)

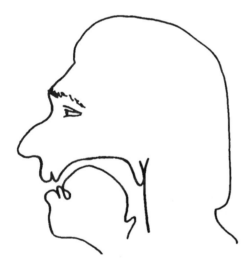

Figure 21. [j]
rayado [ra'jaðɔ]

This is a sound identical to the sound of the *y* in the English word *yes.* It is a voiced palatal fricative. The lips adopt the position of the vowel that follows. The tip of the tongue leans on the lower incisors, and the back rises in a convex form, touching the palate on both sides of the mouth and forming a large opening in the middle, through which the air escapes. This sound occurs in initial position, and in interior position in a word or word group, as long as it is not preceded by *l* or *n*, in which case it becomes the [dʒ] affricate described above.

Speak and then sing the following examples:

de hierro	[dɛ'jɛrrɔ]	(made of iron)
rayado	[ra'jaðɔ]	(scratched)
hoyo	['ɔjɔ]	(hole)
mi yerno	[mi'jɛrnɔ]	(my brother-in-law)
la hiel	[la'jɛl]	(the bile)
mi hielo	[mi'jɛlɔ]	(my ice)

The Palatal Nasal [ɲ]   (Written ñ)

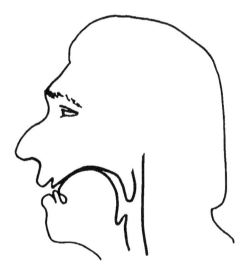

Figure 22. [ɲ]
niño ['niɲɔ]

This is a voiced nasal palatal (it has a vocal sound, nasal resonance, and involves the hard palate). The tip of the tongue leans on the lower incisors, and the top of it touches the hard palate with its full width. The soft palate is open, and as the tongue totally blocks the mouth opening, the escaping air exits through the nose. It is the same sound as in the Italian *ogni*. English speakers can make this sound by greatly exaggerating the second syllable of *canyon*.

Speak and then sing the following examples:

niña	['niɲa]	(young girl)
piña	['piɲa]	(pineapple)
riña	['riɲa]	(squabble)
pequeño	[pe'keɲɔ]	(small)
España	[ɛs'paɲa]	(Spain)
maña	['maɲa]	(trick)
puño	['puɲɔ]	(fist)
peña	['peɲa]	(rock)
paño	['paɲɔ]	(cloth)

The Palatal Lateral [ʎ]   (Written *ll*)

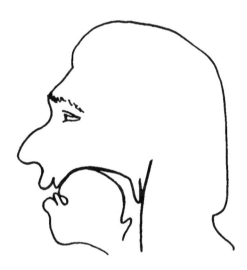

Figure 23. [ʎ]
calle ['kaʎe]

This is a voiced lateral palatal sound. The tip of the tongue touches the lower incisors. The top of the tongue, as with [ɲ], makes wide contact with the palate. At the sides of the mouth (ergo, lateral), the tongue separates from the back molars and creates a narrow opening at each side, through which the air escapes. The same sound occurs in Italian in such words as *figlio* and *moglie*. In Castillian Spanish, this is a widely used sound, although in Latin American Spanish, it is not used at all (see Chapter 11 — Latin American Variants).

Speak and then sing the following examples:

llevar	[ʎeˈβar]	(to take)
llenar	[ʎeˈnar]	(to fill)
llamar	[ʎaˈmar]	(to call)
llave	[ˈʎaβe]	(key)
llorar	[ʎɔˈɾar]	(to weep)
lluvia	[ˈʎuβja]	(rain)
escollo	[esˈkɔʎɔ]	(reef)
tortilla	[tɔrˈtiʎa]	(omelet)
amarillo	[amaˈɾiʎɔ]	(yellow)
pollo	[ˈpoʎɔ]	(chicken)
estrella	[esˈtɾeʎa]	(star)

If you find it difficult to make this sound, an acceptable option is to say [l] and [j] in quick succession, thus: [lj]. One could settle for *amarillo* pronounced [amaˈɾiljɔ], but certainly not [amaˈɾiliɔ]. Note than even in Spain, there is wide acceptance of a variant to the above [ʎ] palatal sound: It is the soft [dj] affricate. Words like *estrella* [esˈtɾeʎa] can be heard as [esˈtɾedja] and *calle* [ˈkaʎe] as [ˈkadje]. However, singers singing Spanish songs from Spain should endeavor to pronounce the double *ll* as [ʎ] or, if necessary, [lj].

Mo- ris - cos de a - llen- de   lo lle - van cau - ti - vo.
mɔ ris   kɔz   ðea   ʎen de   lɔ ʎe   βan kau   ti   βɔ

Musical Example 16

From "Ay que no hay"
Anonymous Moorish villancico, XV Century

VELAR CONSONANTS [k], [g], [ɣ], [ŋ], [x]

The Velar Plosive [k]   (Written *qu*, *k* or *c*)

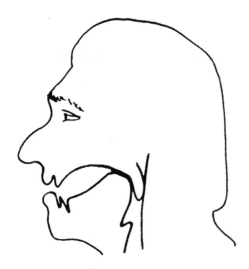

Figure 24. [k], [g]
carro ['karrɔ]
ganar [ga'nar]

This is a voiceless velar plosive (no vocal sound, the velum or soft palate is involved, and it is created by an explosion of air). To make this sound, the back of the tongue rises towards the velum, or soft palate, closing off the flow of air. The tip of the tongue lowers almost to the gums of the lower incisors. As with the [t] and [p] plosives, [k] must be unaspirated, and no puff of air should be allowed to escape between the explosion of the consonant and the sound that follows.

Speak and then sing the following examples:

[k] written *qu* (before *e* or *i*):

quiso	['kisɔ]	(he wanted)
quieto	['kjetɔ]	(quiet)
quitar	[ki'tar]	(take away)
querer	[ke'rer]	(to want)
quince	['kinθε]	(fifteen)
quemar	[ke'mar]	(to burn)
querido	[ke'riðɔ]	(beloved)

The [k] sound is written as a *k* only in non-Spanish words.

[k] written *k:*

kilómetro	[ki'lɔmɛtrɔ]	(kilometer)
kilogramo	[kilo'ɣramɔ]	(kilogram)
kilolitro	[kilo'litrɔ]	(kiloliter)
whisky	['wiski]	(whisky)

[k] written *c* (before *a, o* or *u*):

casa	['kasa]	(house)
cama	['kama]	(bed)
comer	[kɔ'mɛr]	(to eat)
comida	[kɔ'miða]	(food)
cuna	['kuna]	(cradle)
cuñado	[ku'ɲaðɔ]	(brother-in-law)

Note that in a cluster with *t*, the [k] sound gets imploded as in American speech, in such words as *actor, fictitious, pact* and *contact.* In Spanish as well, it is the following *t* that gets most of the explosive quality.

[k] in cluster with *t:*

actor	['a(k)tɔr]	(actor)
pacto	['pa(k)tɔ]	(pact)
invicto	[im'bi(k)tɔ]	(undefeated)
pectoral	[pɛ(k)tɔ'ral]	(pectoral)
tractor	['tra(k)tɔr]	(tractor)

The Velar Plosive [g]   (Written *g* or *gu*)

This is a velar voiced plosive. There is less tension than for [k] because of voicing; otherwise, all organs are in identical position (see Figure 24). It occurs in absolute initial position, written as *g* before *a, o* or *u,* and *gu* before *e* or *i.*

Speak and then sing the following examples:

[g] written *g* before *a, o* and *u:*

gato	['gatɔ]	(cat)
ganar	['ganar]	(to win)
goma	['gɔma]	(rubber)
gorro	['gɔrrɔ]	(cap)
gusto	['gustɔ]	(taste)
gusano	[gu'sanɔ]	(worm)

[g] written *gu* before *e* and *i:*

guiso	['gisɔ]	(stew)
guitarra	[gi'tarra]	(guitar)
guerra	['gɛrra]	(war)
guillotina	[giʎɔ'tina]	(guillotine)

The [g] sound is also used in an interior position in a word or word group when *g* is preceded by a nasal consonant.

[g] preceded by a nasal:

rango	['raŋgɔ]	(rank)
rengo	['rɛŋgɔ]	(lame)
pongo	['pɔŋgɔ]	(I put)
un grado	[uŋ'graðɔ]	(one grade)
ingrato	[iŋ'gratɔ]	(ingrate)
engrase	[ɛŋ'grasɛ]	(grease job)
engaño	[ɛŋ'gaɲɔ]	(deceit)
un guante	[uŋ'gwantɛ]	(one glove)
un gorro	[uŋ'gɔrrɔ]	(one cap)

The Velar Fricative [ɣ]   (Written *g* or *gu*)

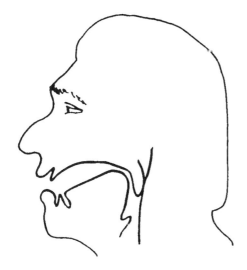

Figure 25. [ɣ]
agua [ˈaɣwa]

This is a voiced velar fricative. The back of the tongue rises against the velum or soft palate as for [g], but without making complete contact. The air escapes through the narrow passage remaining, causing a soft friction. All *g*'s, unless they are in absolute initial position or after a nasal *n* as shown above, become the soft fricative [ɣ]. The same happens to *gu* in an interior position when it precedes *e* or *i*.

Speak and then sing the following examples:

[ɣ] written *g* before *a, o* and *u:*

arruga	[aˈrruɣa]	(wrinkle)
llegada	[ʎeˈɣaða]	(arrival)
hogar	[ɔˈɣar]	(home)
alegre	[aˈleɣɾe]	(happy)
agradable	[aɣɾaˈðaβle]	(agreeable)
digno	[ˈdiɣnɔ]	(worthy)
resignar	[rɛsiɣˈnar]	(resign)
dogmático	[dɔɣˈmatikɔ]	(dogmatic)

[ɣ] written *gu* before *e* and *i:*

águila	['aɣila]	(eagle)
alguien	['alɣjɛn]	(someone)
higuera	[i'ɣɛɾa]	(fig tree)
seguidilla	[sɛɣi'diʎa]	(Sp. dance)
seguir	[sɛ'ɣir]	(to follow)
la guitarra	[laɣi'tarra]	(the guitar)
la guerra	[la'ɣɛrra]	(the war)

De - ba - jo de un li - món   ver- de don- de el a - gua no co - rri - a
de βa   xo ðeun li mom   ber ðɛ   don dɛ   la ɣwa nɔ kɔ   rri   a

Musical Example 17
From "Triste"
by Alberto Ginastera

The Medio-Palatal-Velar Nasal [ŋ]   (Written *n*)

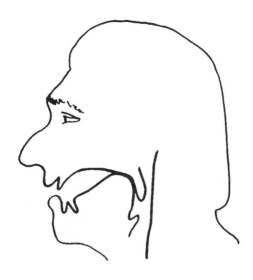

Figure 26. [ŋ]
vengo ['bɛŋgɔ]

This is a voiced medio-palatal-velar nasal (half-way up the hard palate towards the velum or soft palate, with nasal resonance). The letter *n*, when it is placed before either of the two velar plosives [g] or [k] or the velar fricative [x], assimilates to an [ŋ] sound, whether it is in a single word or a group of words. Compare to the English words *fink, hank, dunh, anguish, languid* and *sanguine*. All those *n* letters are in fact an [ŋ] sound. The tongue is raised against the soft palate, and contrary to a normal [n] sound, the tip of the tongue does not touch the ridges of the upper teeth. The soft palate is open in back, allowing the column of air to rise into the nasal cavities and give us the nasal resonance.

Speak and then sing the following examples:

cinco	[ˈθiŋkɔ]	(five)
banco	[ˈbaŋkɔ]	(bank)
rango	[ˈraŋgɔ]	(rank)
pongo	[ˈpɔŋgɔ]	(I put)
hongo	[ˈɔŋgɔ]	(mushroom)
fingir	[fiŋˈxir]	(to fake)
enjambre	[eŋˈxambrɛ]	(swarm)
ronco	[ˈrɔŋkɔ]	(hoarse)
bronca	[ˈbrɔŋka]	(anger)
en cual	[eŋˈkwal]	(in which)
sin querer	[siŋkɛˈrer]	(unwittingly)
con calma	[kɔŋˈkalma]	(with calm)
con ganas	[kɔŋˈganas]	(with gusto)

Con   qué   la   la - va - re
kɔŋ   kɛ   la   la - βa - rɛ

Musical Example 18

From "Con qué la lavaré"
from *Cuatro Madrigales Amatorios* by Joaquín Rodrigo

The Velar Fricative [x]   (Written *j* or *g)*

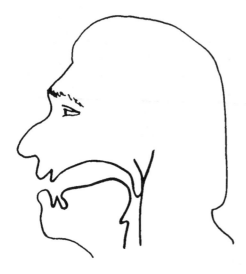

Figure 27. [x]
jota ['xɔta]

This is a voiceless velar fricative (no vocal sound, produced as the back of the tongue touches the velum or soft palate, producing friction). The back of the tongue rises against the soft palate without totally blocking the air flow, causing a friction of air. The tip of the tongue, as with all other velar consonants, lowers to below the lower incisors. It is identical to the German *ach* sound in such words as *Bach, doch, Buch* and *auch.*

Speak and then sing the following examples:

[x] written *j* before *a, o* and *u:*

jarra	['xarra]	(jug)
jumento	[xu'mentɔ]	(donkey)
navaja	[na'βaxa]	(razor)
jugar	[xu'ɣar]	(to play)
juzgar	[xuð'ɣar]	(to judge)
dejar	[dɛ'xar]	(to leave)
oreja	[ɔ'rɛxa]	(ear)
oveja	[ɔ'βɛxa]	(sheep)
hija	['ixa]	(daughter)
cojo	['kɔxɔ]	(limping)
rojo	['rɔxɔ]	(red)
reja	['rɛxa]	(grate)

[x] written *g* before *e* and *i:*

regir	[rɛ'xir]	(to reign)
gemir	[xɛ'mir]	(to moan)
girasol	[xira'sɔl]	(sunflower)
fingir	[fiŋ'xir]	(to fake)
general	[xɛnɛ'ral]	(general)
gemelo	[xɛ'mɛlɔ]	(twin)
generoso	[xɛnɛ'rɔsɔ]	(generous)
genio	['xɛnjɔ]	(genius)
gelatina	[xɛla'tina]	(gelatin)
gente	['xɛntɛ]	(people)
gentil	[xɛn'til]	(gentle)

Note that the [x] sound used in Castillian Spanish is greatly softened almost to an [h] sound in Latin American speech (see Chapter 11 — Latin American Variants).

CHAPTER 7

Stress and Accent

In some languages, the stressed or accented syllable always falls on the last syllable, as in French. In Finnish or Hungarian, it usually falls on the first syllable. Then there are languages in which the stress is variable, as in English. Consider the following pairs of words:

con<u>tent</u>	con<u>tent</u>
add<u>ress</u>	add<u>ress</u>
<u>im</u>port	im<u>port</u>
<u>pro</u>duce	pro<u>duce</u>
<u>per</u>mit	per<u>mit</u>
re<u>sume</u>	re<u>sume</u>
<u>con</u>test	con<u>test</u>

By shifting the stress on the underlined syllables, the words acquire different meanings. Spanish, too, has variable stress, but unlike English (or Italian), Spanish has written accents (á, é, í, ó, ú) to aid in identifying the stressed syllable.

Spanish words are classified, according to the placement of the stressed syllable, as oxytones, paroxytones, proparoxitones and superproparoxitones.

Oxytones
(in Spanish, *agudas* or *oxítonas*)

The stress is on the last syllable. Words that end in consonants other than *n* and *s* (unless a written accent is used to specify otherwise) are oxytones.

Speak and then sing the following examples:

hablar	[aˈβlar]	(to speak)
comer	[kɔˈmɛr]	(to eat)
dormir	[dɔrˈmir]	(to sleep)
esperar	[ɛspeˈɾar]	(to sleep)
mamá	[maˈma]	(mother)
corazón	[kɔɾaˈθɔn]	(heart)
están	[ɛsˈtan]	(they are)
atrás	[aˈtras]	(behind)
unión	[uˈnjɔn]	(union)

Paroxytones
(in Spanish, *llanas* or *paroxítonas*)

The stress is on the penultimate syllable (next to the last). All words ending in vowels or the consonants *n* and *s* (unless a written accent is used to specify otherwise) are paroxytones. This is the most common type of Spanish word, and therefore, no written accents are needed.

Speak and then sing the following examples:

canto	[ˈkantɔ]	(I sing)
esta	[ˈɛsta]	(this f.)
auto	[ˈautɔ]	(car)
casa	[ˈkasa]	(house)
partida	[parˈtiða]	(departure)
comida	[kɔˈmiða]	(food)
muchacha	[muˈtʃatʃa]	(girl)
hermano	[ɛrˈmanɔ]	(brother)
España	[ɛsˈpaɲa]	(Spain)

Proparoxytones
(in Spanish, *esdrújulas* or *proparoxítonas*)

The stress is on the antepenultimate syllable (or third to last). All words belonging to this group will have a written accent on the stressed syllable.

Speak and then sing the following examples:

América	[a'mɛɾika]	(America)
teléfono	[te'lefɔnɔ]	(telephone)
kilómetro	[ki'lɔmɛtrɔ]	(kilometer)
rápido	['rapiðɔ]	(quick)
cámara	['kamaɾa]	(camera)
gramática	[gɾa'matika]	(grammar)
sintético	[sin'tɛtikɔ]	(synthetic)
simbólico	[sim'bɔlikɔ]	(symbolic)
perdóname	[pɛr'ðɔnamɛ]	(forgive me)

Superproparoxytones
(in Spanish, *sobreesdrújulas* or *superproparoxítonas*)

The stress is on the pre-antepenultimate syllable (fourth to last). These are usually composite words, and a written accent is needed to show the stressed syllable, just as with proparoxytones.

Speak and then sing the following examples:

cántamela	['kantamɛla]	(sing it to me)
cómetelo	['kɔmɛtɛlɔ]	(eat it up)
impóngaselo	[im'pɔŋgasɛlɔ]	(impose it on him)
cuéntamelo	['kwɛntamɛlɔ]	(tell it to me)

Stress and Meaning

Notice how a written accent that changes the stressed syllable also changes the meaning of the word:

peso	(a weight)	pesó	(he weighed)
bailo	(I dance)	bailó	(he danced)
calle	(street)	callé	(I kept quiet)
libro	(book)	libró	(he freed)
radio	(radio)	radió	(irradiated)
hablo	(I speak)	habló	(he spoke)
canto	(I sing)	cantó	(he sang)

Following is a group of words with stresses on the antepenultimate (proparoxytonic), penultimate (paroxytonic) and last (oxytonic) syllables. Notice how the pronunciation changes their meanings:

Proparoxytones	Paroxytones	Oxytones
término	termino	terminó
(termination)	(I finish)	(he finished)
célebre	celebre	celebré
(famous)	(may he celebrate)	(I celebrated)
límite	limite	limité
(limit)	(may he limit)	(I limited)
depósito	deposito	depositó
(deposit)	(I deposit)	(he deposited)
íntimo	intimo	intimó
(intimate)	(I intimate)	(he intimated)

Note that the middle group does not need an accent, as it belongs to the paroxytonic group. It has a *stress* on the penultimate syllable, but no written accent.

CHAPTER 8

Weakening

A basic characteristic of the English language, as spoken in America, is that the pronunciation of its vowels changes in unstressed syllables in words or word groups. American English "weakens" its unstressed syllables, a phenomenon also called muting. A simple word like *opera*, when pronounced by an American, will come out sounding like ['ɔpɹə], with the second syllable eliminated entirely and the last syllable reduced to a neutral [ə].

In Spanish, all syllables are strong, even the ones in an unstressed position. Thus, in a word like *teléfono*, even though the *lé* syllable is the stressed one in this proparoxytone, the remaining syllables have to be clearly pronounced and given their distinctive qualities, rather than be reduced to neutral sounds.

Pronounce the following similar words in English and Spanish, making sure that no weakening occurs in any of the Spanish unstressed syllables:

per-so-na-li-ty	per-so-na-li-dad
te-le-phone	te-lé-fo-no
te-le-vi-sion	te-le-vi-sión
la-bo-ra-to-ry	la-bo-ra-to-rio
im-pres-sive	im-pre-sio-nan-te
con-ver-sa-tion	con-ver-sa-ción
ir-res-pon-si-bi-li-ty	ir-res-pon-sa-bi-li-dad
ve-te-ri-na-ry	ve-te-ri-na-rio

Note that in fast conversational Spanish, as in all languages, there will be a certain amount of weakening. However, in singing, where every syllable is assigned a sung note, the singer must avoid weakening syllables.

Practice the following phrase in de Falla's "Seguidilla Murciana." Do not weaken any of the syllables, especially the ones that are not on a strong musical beat.

Musical Example 19

From "Seguidilla Murciana"

from *Siete Canciones Populares Españolas* by Manuel de Falla

CHAPTER 9

Assimilation

Sometimes a consonant, due to the type of consonant following it, assumes the qualities of that neighbor. This is called assimilation. We find this quite often in Italian and Spanish, where, in a common phrase like *un momento*, the *n* of *un* "assimilates" with the initial *m* of *momento*, and we invariably hear, in both languages, *ummomento* [ummɔ'mentɔ].

There is assimilation in English as well. Try this experiment: Say *one time* and notice that, on the *n* of *one*, the tongue touches the inside of the upper teeth, preparing to say *time*. Now say *one thing* and notice that this time, on the *n* of *one*, the tongue assumes an interdental position to get ready to say *thing*, which begins with the interdental [θ] sound.

There are dozens of such assimilations in all languages, and we are almost never aware of them. In Spanish, we must talk about three of these *n* assimilations and one *s* assimilation, which are necessary for correct idiomatic Spanish singing.

n before [m], [b] or [p] = [m]

When *n* precedes a bilabial consonant [m], [b] or [p] in a word or word group in a breath phrase, it will cease being articulated as a dental [n] consonant and assume the bilabial position of [m]. It will be written phonetically as [m].

In the following musical example, notice the assimilation of *n* before [p] in *con peseta* and before [m] in *de mano en mano*.

Musical Example 20

From "Seguidilla Murciana"
from *Siete Canciones Populares Españolas* by Manuel de Falla

Assimilation makes the singing of these words and phrases much more idiomatic and simple. Other combinations of words that involve such an assimilation are:

un poco	[um'pɔkɔ]	(a little)
un buen dia	[um'bwɛn'dia]	(a good day)
en mi pecho	[ɛmmi'petʃɔ]	(in my breast)
un pedazo	[umpɛ'daθɔ]	(a piece)
un beso	[um'bɛsɔ]	(a kiss)

Musical Example 21

From "Con qué la lavaré"
from *Cuatro Madrigales Amatorios* by Joaquín Rodrigo

n before [k], [g] or [x] = [ŋ]

When *n* precedes a velar consonant — either [k], [g] or the [x] fricative — it assimilates to the mediopalatal [ŋ] sound. This is the same assimilation that occurs in English in such words as *bank, stink, dunk, longing* and *languish.* In Italian, the same thing occurs in words like *stanco, sangue* and *ancora.* Note as well the following examples of assimilation:

cinco	['θiŋkɔ]	(five)
banco	['baŋkɔ]	(bank)
blanco	['blaŋkɔ]	(white)
enjambre	[eŋ'xambre]	(swarm)
enjuagar	[eŋxwa'ɣar]	(to soak)
sangre	['saŋgre]	(blood)
engreído	[eŋgre'iðɔ]	(conceited)
ingreso	[iŋ'gresɔ]	(entrance)

In the following musical examples, note the assimilation of *n* before the [k] sound of *dicen que* and *aunque,* and before the [x] sound of *en Jaén.*

Musical Example 22
From "Jota"
by Manuel de Falla

Musical Example 23
From "Tres Morillas"
Anonymous Moorish villancico, XV Century

n before [f] = [ɱ]

The letter *n*, when it precedes the labiodental [f], also assumes a labiodental position and becomes [ɱ], as in the following words and phrases:

infierno	[iɱˈfjɛrnɔ]	(hell)
en favor	[ɛɱfaˈβɔr]	(in favor)
confiar	[kɔɱˈfiar]	(to trust)
con fervor	[kɔɱferˈβɔr]	(with fervor)
un favor	[uɱfaˈβɔr]	(a favor)
infeliz	[iɱfɛˈliθ]	(unhappy)
infantil	[iɱfanˈtil]	(infantile)
con furia	[kɔɱˈfurja]	(with fury)

Notice the assimilation in this musical example from Antonio Literes' "Confiado Jilguerillo":

Musical Example 24
From "Confiado Jilguerillo"
from heroic zarzuela *Acis y Galatea* by Antonio Literes

s before a voiced consonant = [z]

The letter *s* loses its voiceless sibilant quality when it precedes a voiced consonant, such as *b, d, g, n, m, l, v* or *r*, in a word or group of words, as in the following examples:

nos vamos	[nɔz'βamɔs]	(we are going)
les debemos	[lɛzðe'βemɔs]	(we owe you)
les ganamos	[lɛzɣa'namɔs]	(we beat them)
los guantes	[lɔz'ɣwantɛs]	(the gloves)
las notas	[laz'nɔtas]	(the notes)
buenas noches	['bwɛnaz'nɔtʃɛs]	(good evening)
buenos dias	['bwɛnɔz'ðias]	(good day)

Notice this assimilation in Joaquín Rodrigo's "Vos me matásteis" (from *Cuatro Madrigales Amatorios*), in which the *s* in *vos* becomes a softer [z] sound, because it is followed by the voiced [m] of the word *me*. Likewise in the same song, the *s* of *riberas* softens to a [z], because it is followed by a voiced [d] of the word *de*.

Musical Example 25

From "Vos me matásteis"
from *Cuatro Madrigales Amatorios* by Joaquín Rodrigo

An *s* before unvoiced consonants, such as [p], [t], [k], [x] and [f], remains an [s] sound.

CHAPTER 10

Syllabification

In Spanish lyric diction, the division of words, or syllabification, for singing usually corresponds to the written syllable division in normal spelling. The singer need only sing the syllable assigned to the printed note.

Spanish syllables tend to be open, beginning with a consonant and ending with a vowel. Some examples are:

casa	ca-sa	(house)
lobo	lo-bo	(wolf)
meta	me-ta	(goal)
maravilla	ma-ra-vi-lla	(marvel)

Consonant Clusters

When the following consonant clusters are between vowels, they are inseparable and form an independent syllable with the vowel that follows:

pr	oprimo	o-pri-mo	(I opress)
br	obrero	o-bre-ro	(laborer)
pl	aplomo	a-plo-mo	(aplomb)
bl	ablandar	a-blan-dar	(to soften)
fr	afrontar	a-fron-tar	(to confront)
gr	lograr	lo-grar	(to achieve)
cl	aclimatizar	a-cli-ma-ti-zar	(acclimatize)
cr	lacre	la-cre	(lacquer)
dr	cuadro	cua-dro	(picture)
tr	cuatro	cua-tro	(four)

Any other consonant pairs between vowels will divide, as in:

| *rt* | artista | ar-tis-ta | (artist) |
| *ns* | inseparable | in-se-pa-ra-ble | (inseparable) |

Multiple Consonants

When three or more consonants appear between two vowels, the following may occur:

(a) When the last two of the three consonants form a syllable in which one of the consonants is a liquid or continuant [l] or [r], they syllabify thus:

inflamar	in-fla-mar	(to inflame)
contraer	con-tra-er	(to contract)
empleados	em-ple-a-dos	(employees)

(b) When the first two consonants are a nasal and an [s], they syllabify thus:

construír	cons-tru-ír	(to build)
instaurar	ins-tau-rar	(to install)
constatar	cons-ta-tar	(to ascertain)

Multiple Vowels

When two or more vowels appear together, the following may occur:

(a) When there is contact between vowels that are not both high vowels [i] or [ɛ], two different syllables are produced:

aéreo	a-é-re-o	(air mail)
pelear	pe-le-ar	(to fight)
beato	be-a-to	(beatific)
poeta	po-et-a	(poet)
poema	po-em-a	(poem)

(b) When an unaccented vowel comes in contact with a vowel that has a written accent, this also results in two syllables:

salía	sa-lí-a	(he was leaving)
reúno	re-ú-no	(I reunite)
baúl	ba-úl	(trunk)
laúd	la-úd	(lute)
comía	co-mí-a	(I was eating)

(c) When there is contact between a back [ɔ] or [u] or mid-vowel [a], and a high [i] or [ɛ], and a diphthong is formed, they create a single syllable:

Europa	Eu-ro-pa	(Europe)
aire	ai-re	(air)
bueno	bue-no	(good)
fuego	fue-go	(fire)
Asia	a-sia	(Asia)

(d) Triphthongs, like diphthongs, form a syllable:

asociais	a-so-ciais	(you associate)
buey	buey	(ox)
apreciais	a-pre-ciais	(you appreciate)
combiaos	com-biaos	(change yourselves)
averigüais	a-ve-ri-güais	(you investigate)

Notice, in the following musical example, how the musical notation simplifies syllabification.

Musical Example 26

From "Canto a la Espada Toledana"
from zarzuela *El Huésped del Sevillano* by Jacinto Guerrero

CHAPTER 11

Latin American Variants

The Spanish language suffered great changes from its voyage across the Atlantic to the New World. Many theories have been advanced to explain this phenomenon, and experts on geographic linguistics and ethnolinguistics have put forth theories that state that the climate of the tropics or the torrid zones of the Equator have made the language "lazy," or that the dizzying heights of the Andes in Peru, Bolivia and Chile have influenced the sounds of plosive and fricative consonants to a degree. The mixing of the races, and elements of Amerindian languages and language sounds from the Americas, plus speech patterns of the transplanted African population, have also had their influence on the Spanish language in the Americas.

It all makes for a fascinating study, but the singer need only be aware of some of the basic differences between high Castillian speech and the more relaxed (and sometimes startling) Latin American variants.

It is generally assumed that Colombia has the best Latin American Spanish in the Americas. Mexico has a decided *cantilena* that rises upward at the end of phrases in a most charming manner, as do Argentina and Cuba. Argentina and Uruguay, along the River Plate estuary, have their decided particularities, but it is the countries of the Caribbean region, including Puerto Rico, Cuba, Santo Domingo and Venezuela, that lead the list with their linguistic relaxation.

Singers singing Latin American music are advised to use Latin American pronunciation. Following are the variations you would do well to incorporate.

Ceceo vs. *Seseo*

The most startling difference which is immediately noticed is the absence of *ceceo* [θɛˈθɛɔ], the lisping [θ] sound of the Spanish *z* and *c* (the latter before *e* and *i*). In Latin America, an *s* is used in both cases. *Zaragoza*, which in Spain is pronounced [θɑrɑˈɣɔθɑ], is pronounced [sɑrɑˈɣɔsɑ] in Latin America. *Cinco* and *cera*, pronounced [ˈθiŋkɔ] and [ˈθɛrɑ] in Spain, are simply pronounced [ˈsiŋkɔ] and [ˈsɛrɑ] in Latin America. This change from the lisping to the nonlisping pattern is called *seseo* [seˈsɛɔ].

The *s* Sound   *spoken only*

Another casualty of the transatlantic voyage is the Spanish predorsal thick *s*, which sounds as if it had some *sh* [ʃ] in it. The *s* used in Latin America is the common dental Italian *s* sound, save for a few pockets of population in the interior sections or the high Andes.

Aspiration or Omission of Final *s*

The letter *s* suffers a great deal of mistreatment: we also find in Latin America the aspiration of *s* or its total disappearance. In the Spanish-speaking Caribbean islands and in large parts of South America, an *s* in a postvocalic position (after the vowel) is mostly aspirated, or replaced by a little *h*, and even at times totally omitted. A phrase like *las cosas buenas* (the good things) would be pronounced *lah cosah buenah*, or in extreme cases of laziness, *la cosa buena*, without even a hint of an *s*.

This, in all fairness, is not a unique Latin American phenomenon. In Andalucía (in southern Spain) and other provinces, the same thing happens. This almost gives credence to the theory that, because Columbus equipped his ships with mostly Andalusian crews from the south, this speech pattern was perpetuated by the Conquistadores in the New World. This cannot be wholly believed, however, because Columbus had crew members from other parts of Spain as well. But perhaps the tropical heat was just too oppressive, and the proud Spanish Conquistadores were conquered by what I call "The Tropical *s* Syndrome." In Latin America the *s*'s that do survive the mayhem are, as noted above, the normal English/Italian/French kind, and not the thick predorsal Castillian type.

Lleísmo vs. *Yeísmo*   Yey

Watch also for the substitution of *yeísmo* for *lleísmo*. As we have seen, the double *ll* consonant, as in *Sevilla, llave, calle* and *amarillo*, is pronounced in Spain as [se'βiʎa], ['ʎaβε], ['kaʎε] and [ama'riʎɔ], with a well-pronounced palatal-lateral [ʎ] sound, the same as the Italian sound in such words as *figlio* and *moglie*. The use of this double *ll* [ʎ] sound (called *elle* ['εʎε] in Spanish) is referred to as *lleísmo* [ʎε'izmɔ].

Sometimes, even in Spain, this [ʎ] sound changes to a soft [dj] affricate, so that *amarillo* would sound like [ama'ridjɔ]. In Latin America, this tendency persists. In Mexico, Central America and regions of South America, where hardly anyone uses the [ʎ] anymore, the *ll* sound is reduced to an even simpler [j] glide, called *yeísmo* [je'izmɔ], so that the word for *chicken (gallina)* would sound like *gayina*, or even *gaína*. It is definitely less muscularly exerting to use the latter pronunciations, and here we see the ever-present theory of the "path of least resistance" taking effect, endeavoring to make the pronunciation of all languages simpler and less exerting.

In the following examples, the words in the left column are pronounced with a *yeísmo* [j] sound. The words in the right column, pronounced in correct Spanish with a *lleísmo* [ʎ] sound, have totally different meanings.

poyo	(a stone bench)	pollo	(chicken)
rayar	(to scratch)	rallar	(to grate)
Maya	(Indian tribe)	malla	(a mesh or T-shirt)
gayo	(grackle)	gallo	(cockerel)
huya	(let him flee)	hulla	(coal)

The meaning of these words has to be deduced from context, but Latin Americans seem to have no problem identifying these similar-sounding words. Only Argentinians and Uruguayans would pronounce words with *ll* much differently, as discussed below.

Argentinian-Uruguayan *Zheísmo* ([ʒɛ'izmɔ])

In parts of Argentina and Uruguay, especially in the River Plate estuary of Buenos Aires and Montevideo, the double *ll* of *calle, Sevilla* and *amarillo* gets pronounced with a palatal [ʒ] sound (like the *s* in *pleasure*), resulting in ['kaʒɛ], [sɛ'βiʒa] and [ama'riʒɔ]. The letter *y* in initial position, as in the pronoun *yo* (I, myself), is pronounced ['ʒɔ]. The letter *y* in interior position, in such words as *hoyo, raya* and *haya*, gets pronounced ['ɔʒɔ], ['raʒa] and ['aʒa]. Keep this in mind when singing songs by Argentinian composers such as Buchardo, Guastavino and Ginastera.

Following are three examples of Argentinian *zheísmo* in song:

Cuan-do can-to cha - ca - re-ras   me dan ga - nas de llo - rar
kwan dɔ kan tɔ   tʃa   ka ɾɛ ɾas   me ðaŋ ga naz ðɛ   ʒɔ   ɾar

Musical Example 27
From "Chacarera"
by Alberto Ginastera

Yo   no te o - frez - co gran - de - zas vi - day
ʒɔ   nɔ teɔ fɾes   kɔ ɣɾan de   saz βi - ðaj

Musical Example 28
From "Desde que te conocí"
by Carlos Guastavino

A u- na rio-ja-na lin- da qe e-lla me qui- so y me e-na-mo - ré
au na rjɔ xa na lin da kɛ ʒa mɛ ki sɔj mɛ na mɔ rɛ

Musical Example 29
From "Viniendo de Chilecito"
by Carlos Guastavino

Other words with *ll* and *y* that suffer the *zheísmo* transformation are:

ayuda	[aˈʒuða]	(help)
ayer	[aˈʒɛr]	(yesterday)
pollera	[pɔˈʒɛra]	(skirt)
playa	[ˈplaʒa]	(beach)
millonario	[miʒɔˈnarjɔ]	(millionaire)
estrella	[ɛsˈtrɛʒa]	(star)
pellejo	[pɛˈʒɛxɔ]	(scalp)

Note that in some cases, there is also a tendency to unvoice the [ʒ] to a *sheísmo* [ʃ] (like the *sh* sound of *cashier*), so that the "normal" (for Argentina!) pronounciation for *calle* [ˈkaʒɛ] would become [ˈkaʃɛ], and the words above would be pronounced [aˈʃuða], [aˈʃɛr], [pɔˈʃɛra], [ˈplaʃa], [miʃɔˈnarjɔ], [ɛsˈtrɛʃa] and [pɛˈʃɛxɔ]. For singers, we advise the voiced and more singable [ʒ] in Argentinian songs.

Reversal of *l* and *r*

In certain Caribbean areas, especially Puerto Rico and Venezuela, there is a marked tendency to reverse the letters *l* and *r*. Most Puerto Ricans refer to their lovely island as *Puelto Rico* and one of their loveliest tropical resorts, Isla Verde, as *Isla Velde*. This occurs even among educated people. In Venezuela, the same thing happens, but not as often among the educated. The reverse substitution also happens, as with the word *alma* (soul), which sometimes transforms into *arma* (which means weapon!). In all frankness, one hears this *l/r* transposition in Gypsy Spanish in southern Spain quite often, and in many zarzuela arias, composers use this for their "Gypsy" or popular class characters.

The Puerto Rican Velar *r*

Not only do Puerto Ricans pronounce their country as *Puelto Rico*, but *Rico*, instead of having a trilled [r] at the beginning, has a velar [x] sound (a sort of "French *r*" pronounced in the back of the throat like the German sound in *Bach)*, resulting in ['xikɔ]. One theory for this is that the Indians and Africans had no such trilled *r* sound, and they came up with the substitute velar sound, which persisted through the centuries and is still used today. The exact same phenomenon occurred in Brazil with the Portuguese trilled *r*, which, for the exact same reasons, transformed into a velar [x] sound.

The Velarized Final *n*

In some countries in Latin America, excluding Mexico, Argentina, Uruguay and Colombia, a final *n* as in *pan* (bread) becomes a velarized [ŋ], and ['pan] becomes ['paŋ]. Words like *común, avión, están, sartén* and *chiquilín* almost always undergo this particular change to [kɔ'muŋ], [a'βjɔŋ], [ɛs'taŋ], [sar'tɛŋ] and [tʃiki'liŋ].

[x] Reduced to [h]

Most Spanish words with a velar fricative [x] sound would be pronounced with a much less tense velar sound, more like an [h]. Words with a *j*, as in *jota, jarabe, jumento, maja* and *abeja*, which in Spain would be pronounced as ['xɔta], [xa'raβɛ], [xu'mɛntɔ], ['maxa] and [a'βexa], soften to ['hɔta], [ha'raβɛ], [hu'mɛntɔ], ['maha] and [a'βɛha]. Words with a *g*, as in *genio, gemir* and *gitano*, pronounced in Spain as ['xɛnjɔ], [xɛ'mir] and [xi'tanɔ], would be pronounced ['hɛnjɔ], [hɛ'mir] and [hi'tanɔ] in most of Latin America.

There are regional variations to this. The River Plate estuary of Argentina and Uruguay gives it a bit harder *h*, somewhere between a relaxed [h] and a harder German [x] as in *Bach*. In Chile, a word like *gente* (people) or *genio* (genius) will be startlingly pronounced ['çente] or ['çenjɔ], with an almost German palatal fricative *ich* [ç] sound. This sound, according to one linguistic theory, is believed to be derived from an Araucanian source (the Amerindians who inhabited Chile before the Spanish arrived), but it has been widely disputed.

Amerindian Derivatives

Throughout Latin American Spanish, words can be found that have come from the Amerindian languages of the continent. In the New World, the Spanish Conquistadores found a new environment, a lush natural habitat with unfamiliar fruits and vegetation, which they started to identify by their native Indian names. Some of the Indian tribes encountered by the Conquistadores were the Arawaks *(Arahuacos)* in the Antilles, the Caribs *(Caribes)* in Venezuela and the Guyanas, the Nahuatl in Mexico, the Quechuas in Peru, the Araucanians in Chile, and the Guaraníes in Paraguay and Brazil. Many words from these languages found their way not only into Spanish, but into English as well.

Following are some examples of these words, listed by the Amerindian language they come from:

ARAWAK (Antilles)

batata	(sweet potato)	tabaco	(tobacco)
hamaca	(hammock)	caníbal	(cannibal)
tiburón	(shark)	yuca	(yucca)
huracán	(hurricane)	guayaba	(guava)
batea	(bathtub)		

NAHUATL (Mexico)

aguacate	(avocado)	cacao	(cocoa)
chocolate	(chocolate)	tomate	(tomato)
cacahuete	(peanut)	hule	(linoleum)
pulque	(fermented drink)	coyote	(coyote)
cuate	(small child)	ocelote	(ocelot)
chile	(chili)		

QUECHUA (Peru)

cóndor	(condor)	llama	(Andean animal)
alpaca	(Andean animal)	vicuña	(Andean animal)
guanaco	(Andean animal)	puma	(cougar, puma)
coca	(coca leaf)	mate	(mate leaf)
pampa	(prairie)		

GUARANÍ (Paraguay & Brazil)

tapir	(So. Amer. mammal)	tapioca	(tapioca)
jaguar	(jaguar)	ananá	(pineapple)
coatí	(So. Amer. mammal)	mucama	(maid)
petunia	(petunia)		

ARAUCANIAN (Chile)

gaucho	(gaucho)	poncho	(poncho)

CHAPTER 12

Ladino — The Ancient Language of the Sephardic Jews of Spain

Despite the controversy that exists as to the actual definition of "Ladino," let us state for the sake of clarity that Ladino, according to the *Diccionario De La Real Academia Española*, is "ancient Castillian." It is also the name of the ancient Judeo-Spanish dialect spoken by the Sephardic (Spanish) Jews in their diaspora. It is not to be confused with Ladin, or Rumansch, the fourth national language of Switzerland, spoken by more than 50,000 Swiss living in the high and low Engandine and Münstertal. That is also a language derived from Latin, although it contains a few Germanic characteristics as well.

The name Ladino (derived from Latino or Latin) was given by medieval Jews of Spain to the language of their prayers. After the Spanish Inquisition expelled the Jews in 1492, the word came to be synonymous with the Spanish language of the exiled Spanish Jews. This ancient language was carried by the exiles to all points of their dispersion, and in time it absorbed many words of Greek, Rumanian, Turkish, Arabic, Slovenian, Portuguese, French and Italian origin, depending on where these Sephardic Jews settled.

Ladino offers the linguist a living panorama of the language spoken in Castille and other parts of the Iberian peninsula during the beginning of the fifteenth century. In the intervening centuries, the Spanish language as it existed in Spain evolved philologically to what it is today, whereas Ladino, throughout the centuries of dispersion, remained linguistically fossilized, so to speak. It has preserved hundreds of archaic Spanish words, most of which have disappeared from use in modern Spanish. The linguistic curiosity seeker will find in this Judeo-Spanish tongue a veritable "El Dorado"

124

of linguistic possibilities for exploration and conjecture.

Some purists dismiss Ladino as a bastard jargon or "bad Spanish," unworthy of being recognized. Today's modern Spanish speaker may find Ladino spelling, phonetics, morphology and syntax somewhat odd, and in their zeal may hasten to "correct" it into modern Spanish. This should not be done! It would be tantamount to having a linguist correct a Yiddish text into modern German or Elizabethan English into modern American prose.

Below is a brief summary of Ladino pronunciation. Keep in mind that it can vary slightly, depending on the country where it was spoken. For example, Sephardic Jews from Turkey may not pronounce some sounds the same as those from Rhodes or Salonica. Moroccan speakers may vary from those of Holland or Yugoslavia. The rules pointed out here are general phonetic precepts, eschewing all minute local variants, for which there is simply no space.

Ladino Pronunciation Guide

In general, Ladino is pronounced like modern Spanish. It retains most of the characteristics of the mother tongue — the soft "interior" [β] - [ð] - [ɣ] fricative consonants, the bright vowels — but it does not use *ceceo*, the lisping [θ] sound of Castillian *c* (before *e* and *i),* and the *z* doesn't get dentalized at all, but preserves a [z] sound, something totally unknown in modern Spanish!

G

The letter *g* (before *e* and *i)* is not a velar [x] sound as in Spanish, but a [dʒ] affricate, as in English *judge* or *jump.* The word *gente* would be pronounced ['dʒɛntɛ], just as in Italian. A *g* before *a, o* or *u* would remain a velar plosive: [ga], [go], [gu].

J

This letter, as in the words *ijo, cortijo, espejo* and *foja*, is again not a velar fricative [x], but a soft voiced palatal [ʒ] sound, as in the French *jour* ['ʒuːr]. The above words would therefore be pronounced ['iʒɔ], [kɔr'tiʒɔ], [ɛs'peʒɔ] and ['fɔʒa]. (See Musical Examples 30 and 32.)

Hi - ja mi	a mi	que - ri - da
i ʒa mi	a mi	kɛ ri ða

Musical Example 30

From "Una matica de ruda"
Traditional Sephardic song

LL

The double *ll* in such words as *ella, estrella, lluvias* and *cavallero* is simply pronounced as a [j] glide in true *yeísmo* fashion, just as in some parts of Latin America. Use the English sound of *yet, you* and *mayor*. In many instances, the words in Ladino are already spelled with a *y*, as in *estreyas, yuvias* and *cavayero*. (See Musical Example 31.)

S

The letter *s*, when it is final, in such words as *las, casas, ijos* and *ducados*, is softened to almost a [z] sound instead of a voiceless sibilant [s]. It also retains its soft quality in the middle of words or word groups, as in *las cosas* [laz'kozaz]. Only when it is initial does it keep its full voiceless [s] quality, as in *solombra, salió* or *siete*.

C

The letter *c* (before *e* and *i*) is not an interdental [θ] sound as in Castillian. It is pronounced the Latin American way, in *seseo* style, as an [s]. Such words as *mancevico, manecer, cielo* and *nací* should be pronounced with an [s] sound, thus: [mansɛ'vikɔ], [manɛ'sɛr], ['sjɛlɔ], [na'si] (see Musical Example 31). A *c* before *a, o* or *u* will remain a hard voiced velar plosive [k] sound as usual: [ka], [kɔ], [ku].

Mo-re - na me	lla -	man yo	blan- ca	na - ci
mɔ rɛ na me	ja	man jɔ	βlaŋ ka	na si

Musical Example 31

From "Morena me llaman"
Traditional Sephardic song

Z

Again, unlike Castillian Spanish, the *z* is not an interdental [θ] sound, but a simple [z] sound, as in English *zebra, zone* and *zenith*. Ladino words like *pozo, mozo* and *dulzor* should be pronounced with a [z] sound, thus: ['pɔzɔ], ['mɔzɔ], [dul'zɔr]. A linguistic curiosity that tends to explain why the [z] sound is prevalent in Ladino and not in the mother tongue is that the Jews of Spain had in their Hebrew alphabet the letter *za'in*, which is a [z] sound and therefore familiar to the Sephardic Jewish speaker, but foreign to the Gentile Spaniards. (See Musical Examples 32 and 35.)

Dur - me	dur - me	he- mo- zo hi - ji - co
dur me	dur me	ɛr mɔ zo i ʒi kɔ

Musical Example 32

From "Durme durme hermozo hijico"
Traditional Sephardic song

X

This letter, whether initial, median or final, is pronounced like a [ʃ] fricative, as in English *shoe, ship* or *sham*. It appears in such Ladino words as *páxaro* (bird), *buxquí* (I looked for), *avrímex* (open up to me) and *abaxar* (to lower), which should be pronounced ['paʃarɔ], [buʃ'ki], [a'vrimeʃ] and [aβa'ʃar].

Ay   a - vri - mex   la   puer - ta
aj   a   vri   meʃ   la   pwɛr ta

Musical Example 33
From "Nani nani"
Traditional Sephardic song

V

The letter *v* in Ladino is not, as in Castillian, a [b] or [β] sound. It retains its labiodental [v] sound, as in English *vine, victory* or *Venus*. In the phrase *venimos a ver* from "Scalerica de Oro," the *v*'s should be pronounced [vɛ'nimɔza'vɛr], and not [ben'imosa'βer], as would be the case in Spanish. Again, the theory as to why Ladino speakers felt comfortable with the [v] sound is that the Hebrew letter *vav*, which is a [v] sound, was already part of the Jewish phonological experience centuries before they came to Iberia.

La   no - via   no tie - ne   di - ne -   ro
la   nɔ vja   nɔ tje nɛ   ði nɛ   rɔ

Musical Example 34
From "Scalerica de oro"
Traditional Sephardic song

Musical Example 35
From "Scalerica de oro"
Traditional Sephardic song

KH

This combination of letters appears in words of Hebrew origin, such as *zekhut* (virtue) or *malakhim* (angels), and should be pronounced as a velar fricative [x] sound, as in German *Bach:* [zə'xut] and [mala'xim].

Ladino Repertoire

There is a vast repertory of Ladino song. Even well-known composers such as Joaquín Rodrigo, Mario Castelnuovo-Tedesco and Joaquín Nin-Culmell have published arrangements of Ladino songs. These are songs dealing with courtship, marriage, pregnancy, death, circumcision, love, disdain and tenderness. They are melodic and in many cases very oriental, with beautiful melismatic passages harking back to Moorish and Near Eastern origins. For the singer interested in acquiring some of this song repertoire, a brief listing of sources follows.

Algazi, Leon. *Quatre Mélodies Judeo-Espagnoles.* Paris: Editions Salabert, 1951.

Alvar, Manuel. *Cantos de Boda Judeo-Españoles.* Madrid: Instituto Arias Montano, 1971.

Bensussim, Menachem. *Seven Sephardic Folksongs*. 1986 manuscript, unpublished.

Braun, Yehezkel. *Seven Sephardic Romances*. Tel Aviv: Music Institute, 1968.

Castel, Nico. *The Nico Castel Ladino Song Book*. Cedarhurst, NY: Tara Publications, 1981.

Castelnuovo-Tedesco, Mario. *Three Sephardic Songs*. Tel Aviv: Israel Music Publications, 1959.

Elias, Pedro. *Siete Canciones Sefardíes*. Madrid: Unión Musical Española, 1985.

Garcia-Morante, Manuel. *40 Canciones Sefardíes*. Barcelona: Casa Beethoven, 1983.

Hemsi, Alberto. *Coplas Sefardíes* (6 vols.). Alexandria, Egypt: Editions Orientales de Musique, 1932, 1933, 1935, 1938.

Levy, Isaac. *Antología de la Liturgia Judeo-Española* (5 vols.). Madrid: Ministerio de Educación y Cultura, (date unknown).

———. *Chants Judéo-Espagnols* (5 vols.). London: World Sephardi Organization, 1959, 1970, 1971.

Neumann, Richard. *Sephardic Songs*. New York: Transcontinental Music Publications, 1982.

Nin-Culmell, Joaquín. *Six Chansons Populaires Sephardiques*. Paris: Max Eschig, 1986.

Pla, Roberto. *Cuatro Canciones Sefardíes*. Madrid: Unión Musical Española, 1965.

Rodrigo, Joaquín. *Cuatro Canciones Sefardíes*. Paris: Max Eschig, 1968.

Seroussi, Edwin. *5 Sephardic Wedding Songs From Bulgaria*. 1982 manuscript. Available from Edwin Seroussi, Rehov Shahal 57/2, Giv'at Mordechai, Jerusalem 93721, Israel.

Sojo, Vicente E. *Nueve Canciones de los Sefardíes de Salónica.* Caracas: Escuela de Música José Angel Lamas, 1964.

Valls, Manuel. *Canciones Sefarditas.* Madrid: Unión Musical Española, 1975.

Zephira, Bracha. *Kolot Rabin (Many Voices).* Tel Aviv: Massada Publications, 1978.

APPENDIX A

Glossary

Affricate: A consonant sound which is a combination of a plosive and a fricative sound, as in *champ, judge*.

Alveolar: Having to do with the gum ridges of the upper teeth. A consonant formed when the tongue tip touches the alveoli or gum ridges of the upper teeth, such as *n, l, s, z*.

Alveoli: The gum ridges of one's teeth.

Amerindian: Having to do with the native American Indians.

Andean: Having to do with the Andes mountain chain in Latin America.

Aspiration: That puff of air between the initial consonant and the following vowel.

Articulation: The manner in which one arranges the speech organs in order to pronounce a sound.

Assimilation: When a consonant acquires the articulatory characteristics of its neighboring consonant.

Back vowel: A vowel that requires the tongue to arch in back, such as *u*.

Bilabial: Having to do with the lips. A consonant which is pronounced with both lips together such as *b, p, m*.

Breath phrase: A group of words sung or spoken in one breath.

Cante Jondo: The throaty, earthy style characteristic of Flamenco singing.

Cantilena: A sort of musical cadence of speech or song.

Ceceo: Use of the lisping interdental *th* sound, as in *thing* or *thumb*, in Castillian Spanish. See also Seseo.

Continuant: A consonant that can be sustained and sung through, including [m], [n], [l], [r], [ʎ], [ŋ] and [ɲ]. See also Liquid consonant.

Dental: Having to do with the teeth. A consonant formed by contact between the tongue and the upper incisors, such as *t, d, n, l.*

Diphthong: A group of two vowels forming a single syllable, as in *ho̲u̲se, ra̲i̲se* or *plo̲y̲,* or a single vowel with two sounds, as in *bone, tame* or *time.*

Fricative: A consonant sound that is produced by means of friction, such as *s, z, f, v, sh.*

Glide: A vowel that "leans onto" or glides into the following vowel, as in *piano* or *fiesta.* See also On-glide and Off-glide.

High back vowel: A vowel, such as *u,* that requires the back of the tongue to arch to its maximum toward the velum.

High front vowel: A vowel, such as *i,* that requires the front of the tongue to rise in the mouth.

Incisors: The front teeth that we use to bite into food — four uppers and four lowers.

Interdental: Between the teeth. A consonant formed by placing the tongue between the teeth, as in *t̲h̲is* or *t̲h̲umb.*

Intervocalic: Between vowels, as the letter *r* in *were.*

IPA: The International Phonetic Alphabet.

Labiodental: Having to do with the lips and teeth. A consonant pronounced with the lower lip (labio) touching the upper incisor teeth (dental), such as *f.*

Lingual: Having to do with the tongue (lingua).

Liquid consonant: The [l] and [ʎ] sounds. See also Continuant.

Lleísmo: Use of the [ʎ] sound for the letter *ll*. See also Yeísmo, Zheísmo, Sheísmo.

Low central vowel: A vowel, such as *a,* that requires the tongue to rest at the bottom of the mouth.

Mandible: The lower jaw.

Melisma: A series of notes sung on a single syllable, especially in the ornamental phrases of Near Eastern or Asian music.

Mid back vowel: A vowel, such as *o,* that requires the back of the tongue to arch slightly toward the velum.

Mid high vowel: A vowel, such as *e,* that requires the middle of the tongue to rise in the mouth.

Molars: The teeth we use to chew food, located at the sides and back of the mouth.

Monophthong: A pure vowel, common in Spanish.

Monosyllabic: Having one syllable.

Nasal: Having to do with the nose, such as a nasal consonant *n* or *m.*

Neumes: A set of signs used in the Middle Ages in written church music to indicate melody, manner of performance, etc.

Off-glide: A glide with emphasis on the first vowel, as in *baile* or *peine.* Also called a falling diphthong.

On-glide: A glide with emphasis on the second vowel, as in *fiesta* or *piano.* Also called a rising diphthong.

Oxytone: In Spanish, a word which has its stress on the last syllable, as in *corazón.*

Palatal: Having to do with the hard roof of the mouth. A consonant formed when the front of the tongue touches the palate, as in *champ* or *canyon.*

Palate: The hard roof of the mouth.

Paroxytone: In Spanish, a word which has its stress on the next to last syllable, as in *comida*.

Plosive: A consonant that is produced with a puff of air, such as *p*, *b*, *t*.

Predorsal: Having to do with the front end of the tongue (predorsum).

Proparoxytone: In Spanish, a word which has its stress on the third to last syllable, usually due to an accent, as in *rápido*.

Quadraphthong: A group of four vowels, in a word or group of words, forming a single syllable. Very rare.

Semiconsonant: The [j] or [w] glide. Also called semivowel. See also Glide.

Semivowel: The [j] or [w] glide. Also called semiconsonant. See also Glide.

Seseo: Use of the simple *s* sound in Latin American Spanish. See also Ceceo.

Sheísmo: Use of the [ʃ] sound for the letter *ll*. See also Lleísmo.

Sibilance: The whistling noise of the letter *s*.

Superproparoxytone: In Spanish, a word which has its stress on the fourth to last syllable, usually a composite word, such as *cuéntamelo*.

Syllabification: The separation of words into syllables.

Syllable: A word or part of a word pronounced with a single uninterrupted sounding of the voice.

Triphthong: A group of three vowels, in a word or group of words, forming a single syllable, as in *how is*.

Unvoiced consonant: A consonant or consonant cluster that can be whispered without the aid of a vocal sound, such as *p*, *t*, *k*, *sh*, *ch*, *s*.

Velar: Having to do with the velum or soft palate. A consonant formed when the back of the tongue touches the velum, such as *k* or *g*.

Velum: The soft, fleshy part of the roof of the mouth, towards the rear, in back of the palate.

Vibrant: A consonant produced by a rapid vibrating movement: the *r* varieties.

Villancico: A rustic poem.

Vocal: Having to do with the voice.

Vocalic: Having to do with vowels or vowel sounds.

Voiced consonant: A consonant or consonant cluster that can only be pronounced with the aid of a vocal sound, such as *b, d, g, v, z, n, m, l.*

Yeísmo: Use of the [j] sound for the letter *ll*. See also Lleísmo.

Zheísmo: Use of the [ʒ] sound for the letter *ll*. See also Lleísmo.

APPENDIX B

Partial Listing of Spanish Vocal Repertoire

Abril, A. *Tres Canciones Españolas*. Madrid: Unión Musica Española, 1964.

———. *Canciones de Valdemosa*. Madrid: Editorial Alpuerto, 1978.

Albeniz, Isaac. *Seis Baladas*. Madrid: Unión Musica Española, 1947.

Bacarisse, Salvador. *Tres Canciones Medioevales*. Madrid: Unión Musica Española, 1947.

———. *Rimas de Bécqer*. Madrid: Unión Musica Española, (date unknown).

Bal y Gay, Jesús. *Romances y Villancicos Españoles del Siglo XVI*. Mexico: Casa de España, 1939.

Benko, Daniel. *Spanish Renaissance Songs for Voice and Guitar*. Budapest: Editio Musica Budapest, 1982.

Bernstein, Leonard. *A Julia de Burgos* (soprano solo). New York: Amberson Enterprises (Boosey), 1977.

Buchardo, Carlos. *Seis Canciones al Estilo Popular*. Buenos Aires: Ricordi, 1950.

Chavez, Carlos. *La Casada Infiel*. New York: International Music Publications (Boosey), 1955.

Dorumsgaard, Arne. *Canzoni Scordate* (10 Early Spanish Songs). Paris: Recital Publications, 1987.

Esplá, Oscar. *Canciones Playeras*. Madrid: Unión Musica Española, 1930.

————. *Lírica Española, Op. 54.* Madrid: Unión Musica Española, 1952.

Falla, Manuel de. *Three Songs.* New York: International Music Publications, 1954.

————. *Siete Canciones Populares Españolas.* Paris: Max Eschig, 1923.

García-Lorca, Federico. *Canciones Españolas Antiguas.* Madrid: Unión Musica Española, 1961.

Gerhard, Roberto. *Six Catalan Folksongs.* New York: Boosey & Hawkes, 1933.

————. *Cantares: Seven Spanish Songs for Voice and Guitar.* London: Mills Music, 1934.

Ginastera, Alberto. *Las Horas de Una Estancia.* New York: Southern Music Publishing, 1945.

————. *Cinco Canciones Argentinas.* Buenos Aires: Ricordi, 1943.

Granados, Enrique. *Tonadillas.* Boca Raton, Fla: Masters Publishers, 1990.

————. *Tonadillas.* New York: International Music Publications, 1952.

Grau, E. *30 Composiciones del Cancionero Español, Siglos XV y XVI.* Buenos Aires: Ricordi, 1937.

Guastavino, Carlos. *Canciones Argentinas.* Buenos Aires: Ricordi, 1953.

Guridi, J. *Seis Canciones Castellanas.* Madrid: Unión Musica Española, 1941.

Halffter, Cristóbal. *Dos Canciones Tristes de Primavera.* Madrid: Unión Musica Española, 1964.

————. *Dos Canciones.* Madrid: Unión Musica Española, 1952.

Halffter, Ernesto. *Dos Canciones.* Paris: Max Eschig, 1928.

Halffter, Rodolfo. *Marinero en Tierra.* Buenos Aires: Ricordi Americana, 1965.

———. *Dos Sonetos*. Madrid: Unión Musica Española, 1962.

Lamaña, José Maria. *Cinco Siglos de Canciones Españolas*. Madrid: Unión Musica Española, 1963.

———. *Canciones de la Andalucía Medioeval y Renacentista, Siglos XIII al XVI*. Madrid: Unión Musica Española, 1976.

Laparra, Raoul. *16 Mélodies sur des Thèmes Populaires Espagnoles*. Paris: Heugel et Cie., 1920.

Lasala, Angel. *Poemas Americanos*. Madrid: Unión Musica Española, 1966.

———. *Cuatro Canciones Españolas*. Madrid: Unión Musica Española, 1966.

Lopez-Artigas, Angeles. *Caminos*. Valencia, Spain: Piles, Editora, 1983.

Milán, Luys. *El Maestro. Composizioni per Voce e Vihuela* (XV and XVI Century Romances and Villancicos). Milano: Suvini Zerboni, 1966.

Montsalvadge, Xavier. *Cinco Canciones Negras*. New York: Southern Music Publishing, 1962.

———. *Canciones para Niños (Lorca texts)*. Madrid: Unión Musica Española, 1964.

———. *Soneto a Manuel de Falla (Lorca text)*. Madrid: Unión Musica Española, 1976.

Nin, Joaquín. *Diez Villancicos Españoles*. Paris: Max Eschig, 1934.

———. *Quatorze Airs Anciens* (2 vols.). Paris: Max Eschig, 1925, 1927.

———. *Vingt Chants Populaires Espagnols* (2 vols.). Paris: Max Eschig, 1923, 1924.

Nin-Culmell, Joaquín. *Quatre Chansons Populaires de Salamanque*. Paris: Max Eschig, 1964.

———. *Douze Chansons Populaires de Catalogne*. Paris: Max Eschig, 1955.

————. *3 Poèmes de Gil Vicente.* Paris: Max Eschig, 1955.

————. *4 Chants Populaires d'Andalousie.* Paris: Max Eschig, 1964.

————. *4 Chants Populaires de Catalogne.* Paris: Max Eschig, 1964.

Obradors, Fernando. *Canciones Clásicas* (4 vols.). Madrid: Unión Musica Española, 1921, 1930.

Orrego-Salas, Juan. *El Alba del Alhelí.* Washington, DC: Pan American Union, 1958.

Osma, Julio. *Songs of my Spanish Soil.* Boston: Boston Music Publications, 1920.

Palau, Manuel. *Del Oriente Lejano* (two songs). Madrid: Unión Musica Española, 1972.

————. *Dos Canciones Amatorias.* Valencia, Spain: Instituto Valenciano de Música, 1974.

Rodrigo, Joaquín. *Cuatro Madrigales Amatorios.* London: J & W Chester Editions, Wm. Hansen, 1960.

————. *Dos Canciones para Cantar a los Niños.* Madrid: Unión Musica Española, 1973.

————. *Cantos de Amor y Guerra.* Madrid: Unión Musica Española, 1969.

————. *Dos Poemas para Canto y Flauta.* Madrid: Unión Musica Española, 1963.

————. *2 Villancicos.* Madrid: J. Rodrigo, 1929.

————. *Trois Chansons.* Paris: Rouart Lerolle & Cie., 1929.

Roma, José Maria. *Canciones Españolas Antiguas* (From XIII to XVIII Centuries). Barcelona: Boileau, 1956.

Sciammarella, Valdo. *Cantigas de Amigo.* Buenos Aires: Ricordi, 1955.

Sor, Fernando. *Seguidillas, for Voice and Guitar.* London: Tecla Editions, 1976.

Tarragó, Graciano. *Canciones Españolas del Renacimiento (1440 -1600).* Madrid: Unión Musica Española, 1963.

Toldrá, Eduardo. *A L'ombra del Lledoner.* Madrid: Unión Musica Española, (date unknown).

Truán, Ernesto. *Cuatro Canciones (Garcia Lorca Texts).* Madrid: Editora Música Moderna, 1965.

Turina, Joaquín. *Tres Arias.* Madrid: Unión Musica Española, 1930.

———. *Tres Sonetos.* Madrid: Unión Musica Española, 1930.

———. *Poema en Forma de Canciones.* Madrid: Unión Musica Española, 1936.

———. *Homenaje a Lope de Vega.* Madrid: Unión Musica Española, 1936.

Sample Spanish Song Texts with IPA Transcription

MANUEL DE FALLA: "Seguidilla Murciana"

Cualquiera que el tejado tenga de vidrio no debe tirar piedras al
[kwal'kjɛɾa 'kɛl tɛ'xaðɔ 'tɛŋga 'ðɛ 'βiðɾjɔ 'nɔ 'ðɛβɛ ti'ɾaɾ 'pjeðras 'al
----
del vecino. Arrieros semos, puede que en el camino nos
'ðɛl βɛ'θinɔ – a'rrjɛɾɔs 'sɛmɔs – 'pweðɛ kɛ'nɛl ka'minɔ 'nɔs
----
encontremos. Por tu mucha inconstancia yo te comparo, con
ɛŋkɔn'tɾɛmɔs – 'pɔɾ 'tu 'mutʃa iŋkɔns'tanθja 'jɔ 'tɛ kɔm'paɾɔ – 'kɔm
----
peseta que corre de mano en mano, que al fin se borra y
pɛ'sɛta 'kɛ 'kɔrrɛ 'ðɛ 'manɔ 'ɛm 'manɔ – 'kɛ 'al 'fin 'sɛ 'βɔrra i
----
creyéndola falsa, nadie la toma.
kɾɛ'jɛndɔla 'falsa – 'naðjɛ 'la 'tɔma]

JOAQUÍN RODRIGO: "Vos me matásteis"

Vos me matásteis, niña en cabello, vos me habeis muerto.
['bɔz 'mɛ ma'tastɛis – 'niɲa 'ɛŋ ka'βɛʎɔ – 'bɔz 'mɛ 'aβɛiz 'mwɛrtɔ –

Riberas de un río, ví moza vírgen niña en cabello.
ri'βɛɾaz 'ðɛ 'un 'riɔ – bi 'mɔθa 'βirxɛn 'niɲa 'ɛŋ ka'βɛʎɔ]

NOTE: *Matásteis* and *habeis* have been transcribed using [ɛi] rather than [ɛj], because the diphthong is elongated over slow notes, more than if spoken.

ALBERTO GINASTERA: "Triste" (Argentina)

Debajo de un limón verde donde el agua no corría, entregué
[deˈβaxɔ ˈðɛ ˈun liˈmɔm ˈbɛrðɛ ˈdɔndɛˈlaɣwa ˈnɔ kɔˈrria – entrɛˈɣɛ

mi corazón a quién no lo merecía – ay triste es el día sin sol,
ˈmi kɔraˈsɔn a ˈkjɛn ˈnɔ ˈlɔ mɛrɛˈsia – ˈaj ˈtristɛs ˈel ˈdia ˈsin ˈsɔl –

triste es la noche sin luna, pero más triste es querer sin esperanza
ˈtristɛz ˈla ˈnɔtʃɛ ˈsin ˈluna – ˈpɛrɔ ˈmas ˈtristɛs kɛˈrer ˈsin ɛspeˈransa

ninguna.
niŋˈguna]

TOMÁS BRETÓN: "Una Morena y una Rubia"
(from zarzuela *La Verbena de la Paloma*)

Una morena y una rubia, hijas del pueblo de Madrid, me dan
[ˈuna mɔˈrɛna ˈjuna ˈrubja – ˈixaz ˈðɛl ˈpweβlɔ ˈðɛ maˈðrið – ˈmɛ ˈdan

el opio con tan gracia que no las puedo resistir. Caigo en sus
ɛˈlɔpjɔ ˈkɔn ˈtan ˈɣraθja ˈkɛ ˈnɔ ˈlas ˈpweðɔ resisˈtir – ˈkajɣɔ ˈen ˈsuz

brazos mal dormido, y cuando llego a despertar, siento un
ˈβraθɔs ˈmal ðɔrˈmiðɔ – i ˈkwandɔ ˈʎɛɣɔ a ðɛspɛrˈtar – ˈsjɛntɔ ˈum

placer inexplicable, y un delicioso bienestar. Algo me
plaˈθɛr inɛkspliˈkaβlɛ – ˈjun dɛliˈθjɔsɔ βjɛnɛsˈtar – ˈalɣɔ ˈmɛ

cuestan mis chulapas, pero la cosa es natural, no han de
ˈkwɛstam ˈmis tʃuˈlapas – ˈpɛrɔ ˈla ˈkɔsa ˈez natuˈral – ˈnɔ ˈan ˈðe

salir a todas horas, con un vestido de percal. Pero también
saˈlir a ˈtɔdas ˈɔras – ˈkɔn ˈum bɛsˈtiðɔ ˈðɛ pɛrˈkal – ˈpɛrɔ tamˈbjɛn

algunas veces, se me ha ocurrido preguntar, si me querrán esas
alˈɣunaz ˈβɛθɛs – ˈsɛ ˈmɛa ɔkuˈrriðɔ prɛɣunˈtar – ˈsi ˈmɛ kɛˈrran ˈɛsas

chiquillas por mi dinero nada más.
tʃiˈkiʎas ˈpɔr ˈmi ðiˈnɛrɔ ˈnaða ˈmas]

BIBLIOGRAPHY

Adler, Kurt. *Phonetic and Diction in Singing.* Minneapolis: University of Minnesota Press, 1967.

Adrados, Francisco. *Lingüística Indoeuropea.* Madrid: Gredos, 1975.

Alarcos Llorach, Emilio. *Fonología Española.* Madrid: Gredos, 1981.

Alcalá Venceslada, Antonio. *Vocabulario Andaluz.* Madrid: Gredos, 1980.

Alonso, Amado. *Estudios Lingüísticos.* Madrid: Gredos, 1967.

————. *Estudios Lingüísticos. Temas Hispanoamericanos.* Madrid: Gredos, 1967.

————. *De la Pronunciación Medioeval a la Moderna del Español.* Madrid: Gredos, 1967.

Alvar, Manuel. *El Dialecto Riojano.* Madrid: Gredos, 1967.

————. *Estructuralismo. Geografía Lingüística y Dialectología Actual.* Madrid: Gredos, 1983.

Alvarez Nazario, Manuel. *La Herencia Lingüística de Canarias en Puerto Rico.* San Juan: Pareja, 1972.

————. *Elementos Afronegroides en el Español de Puerto Rico.* San Juan: Pareja, 1972.

Aretz, Isabel. *El Folklore Musical Argentino.* Buenos Aires: Ricordi Americana, 1952.

Armatto de Wetti, Zulema. *Diccionario Guaraní de Usos.* Buenos Aires: Fundación Ross, (date unknown).

Armistead, S. G. *Tres Calas del Romancero Sefardí.* Valencia: Castalia, 1979.

Arquint, Jachen Curdin. *Vierv Ladin. Grammatica Elementara dal Rumansch.* Zürich: Lia Rumantscha, 1964.

Baldinger, Curt. *La Formación Lingüística en Iberia.* Madrid: Gredos, 1972.

Barrocas, David. *Ladino, Judezmo & Spanish-Jewish Dialect.* New York: Foundation for Sephardic Studies, 1976.

Behague, Gerard. *La Música en Latino-América.* Caracas: Monte Avila Editores, 1983.

Beinhauer, Werner. *El Humorismo en el Español Hablado.* Madrid: Gredos, 1973.

———. *El Español Coloquial.* Madrid: Gredos, 1978.

Benardete, José Mair. *Hispanic Culture of the Sephardic Jews.* New York: Hispanic Institute of USA, 1952.

Bodmer, Frederick. *The Loom of Language.* New York: Norton, 1944.

Bynon, Theodora. *Lingüística Histórica.* Madrid: Gredos, 1981.

Canfield, D. Lincoln. *Spanish Pronunciation in the Americas.* Chicago: Chicago University Press, 1981.

Carpenter, Alejo. *La Música en Cuba.* Caracas; Editora Tierra Firme, 1945.

Castel, Nico. *The Nico Castel Ladino Song Book.* Cedarhurst, NY: Tara Publications, 1981.

Catalán, Diego. *Lingüística Ibero-Románica.* Madrid: Gredos, 1974.

———. *Las Lenguas Circumvecinas del Castellano.* Madrid: Paraninfo, 1989.

Corominas, Joan. *Breve Diccionario Etimológico Castellano.* Madrid: Gredos, 1987.

Chase, Gilbert. *Spanish Music.* New York: Dover, 1959.

Cobos, Rubén. *Dictionary of New Mexico and Southern Colorado Spanish.* Santa Fe, NM: Museum of New Mexico Press, 1983.

Colomer, Edmon. *The Singers' Anthology of Twentieth Century Spanish Song.* New York: Helion Press, 1987.

Colorni, Evelina. *Singers' Italian.* New York: G. Schirmer, 1970.

Corominas, Joan. *Tópica Hespérica.* (2 vols.). Madrid: Gredos, 1972.

Coseriu, Eugenio. *Estudios de Lingüística Románica.* Madrid: Gredos, 1977.

Crannell, Kenneth. *Voice and Articulation.* Belmont, CA: Wadsworth Publications, 1990.

Criville y Bragallo, Josep. *Historia de la Música Española.* Madrid: Alianza Música, 1983.

Crystal, David. *Encyclopedia of Language.* Cambridge: Cambridge University Press, 1987.

Cusihuamán, Antonio. *Gramática Quechua Cuzco-Collao.* Lima: Ministerio de Educación, 1976.

De Augusta, Fray Felix Luis. *Diccionario Araucano.* Temuco, Chile: Editorial Kushe, 1991.

De Kock, Josse. *Introducción a la Lingüística Automática en las Lenguas Románicas.* Madrid: Gredos, 1974.

De Granada, Germán. *Estudios Lingüísticos Hispánicos, Afro-hispanos y Criollos.* Madrid: Gredos, 1978.

Diez, Miguel. *Las Lenguas de España.* Madrid: Ministerio de Educación, 1980.

Fernandez de la Cuesta, Ismael. *Historia de la Música Española* (Beginning to Ars Nova). Madrid: Alianza Música, 1983.

Gallo, Cristino. *The Language of the Puerto Rican Street.* San Juan, PR: Cristino Gallo, 1980.

Galmes de Fuente, Alvaro. *Dialectología Mozárabe*. Madrid: Gredos, 1983.

Gili Gaya, Samuel. *Elementos de Fonética General*. Madrid: Gredos, 1978.

Gobello, José. *Diccionario Lunfardo*. Buenos Aires: Peña Lillo, 1978.

Gomez Amat, Carlos. *Historia de la Música Española*. Madrid: Alianza Música, 1983.

Hayes, Curtis W.; Ornstein, Jacob; Gage, William W. *The ABC's of Language and Linguistics*. Lincolnwood, Ill: Voluntad Publications, 1989.

Heffner, R. M. S. *General Phonetics*. Madison, Wisc: University of Wisconsin Press, 1952.

Jaspersen, Otto. *Language — Its Nature, Development and Origins*. New York: Norton, 1964.

Laird, Charlton. *The Miracle of Language*. New York: Fawcett, 1953.

Lehmann, Winifred P. *Introducción a la Lingüística Histórica*. Madrid: Gredos, 1969.

Lopez-Calo, José. *Historia de la Música Española* (XVII Century). Madrid: Alianza Música, 1983.

Marco, Tomás. *Historia de la Música Española* (XX Century). Madrid: Alianza Música, 1983.

Martin-Moreno, Antonio. *Historia de la Música Española* (XVIII Century). Madrid: Alianza Música, 1983.

Martinez-Celdrán, Eugenio. *Fonética*. Barcelona: Teide, 1984.

Meyer-Lübke, Wilhelm. *Romanisches Etymologisches Wörterbuch*. Heidelberg: Karl Winter Verlag, 1972.

Morales, Francisco. *Las Lenguas de España*. Madrid: Ministerio de Educación, 1980.

Navarro, Tomás. *Manual de Pronunciación Española*. Madrid: Raycar S.A., 1982.

Pascual-Recuero, Pascual. *Diccionario Básico Ladino-Español.* Barcelona: Ameller, 1977.

Patt, Chris. *El Anglicismo en el Español Actual Contemporáneo.* Madrid: Gredos, 1980.

Pei, Mario. *The History of Language.* New York: American Library, 1984.

Pitchardo, Esteban. *Diccionario de Frases y Voces Cubanas.* Habana: Editorial Ciencias Sociales, 1985.

Potter, Simeon. *Modern Linguistics.* New York: Norton, 1964.

Pottier, Bernard. *Lingüística Moderna y Filología Hispánica.* Madrid: Gredos, 1976.

Pullum, Geoffrey K.; Ladusaw, William A. *Phonetic Symbol Guide.* Chicago: Chicago University Press, 1986.

Quilis, Antonio; Fernandez, Joseph A. *Curso de Fonética y Fonología Española.* Madrid: Consejo Superior de Investigaciones Científicas, 1982.

Rosetti, A. *Introdução à Fonètica.* Sintra, Portugal: Editora Europa-América, 1974.

Rubio, Samuel. *Historia de la Música Española* (Ars Nova to 1600). Madrid: Alianza Música, 1983.

Sabin, Angel. *Las Lenguas de España.* Madrid: Ministerio de Educación, 1980.

Saldivar, Gabriel. *Historia de la Música en Mexico.* Mexico City: Editora Bellas Artes, 1934.

Sanchez Romero, Antonio. *El Villancico.* Madrid: Gredos, 1969.

Santamaria, Francisco. *Diccionario de Mejicanismos.* Mexico City: Porrúa, 1978.

Saussure, Ferdinand de. *Curso de Linguística General.* Buenos Aires: Losada, 1984.

Sobrer, Josep Miquel. *The Singers' Anthology of Twentieth Century Spanish Song.* New York: Helion Press, 1987.

Tejera, Maria Josefina. *Diccionario de Venezolanismos.* Caracas: Academia General de la Lengua, 1983.

Tió, Salvador. *Sobre el Español de Aquí y Allá.* Rio Piedras, PR: Editorial Plaza Mayor, 1991.

Tovar, Antonio. *Catálogo de las Lenguas de América del Sur.* Madrid: Gredos, 1984.

Von Wartburg, Walter. *La Fragmentación Lingüística en la Romania.* Madrid: Gredos, 1979.

Wall, Joan; Caldwell, Robert; Gavilanes, Tracy; Allen, Sheila. *Diction for Singers.* Dallas: pst...Inc., 1990.

Zamora, Vicente Alonso. *Dialectología Española.* Madrid: Gredos, 1979.

INDEX

Page numbers in **bold** indicate the primary descriptions of those letters and IPA sounds.

About the Author

Nico Castel was born in Lisbon, Portugal, to a set of multilingual parents who inculcated in him, practically from the cradle, the love of languages. His first language was German, learned from his Viennese nanny. Then came Portuguese. When the family moved to Caracas, Venezuela, he learned Spanish and went to a French school. When he was fourteen, his father taught him English, and later, when he became involved in singing, he had no difficulty assimilating Italian.

Singing and languages have been his perennial loves. Now celebrating his twenty-fifth season at the Metropolitan Opera as a distinguished character tenor commanding over 200 operatic roles, and also on that institution's staff as a multilingual style and diction coach for the last fifteen years, Mr. Castel is also a professor of his subject at the New York faculties of the Juilliard School, the Manhattan School of Music and Mannes College, where, in the coming year, he is presenting a year-long course on Spanish and Hispanic vocal literature spanning music from the *Cantigas* of Alfonso El Sabio to contemporary Latin American music. He is an adjunct professor at Boston University and New England Conservatory and a visiting professor at music schools and conservatories throughout the country, including the University of Maryland, Eastman, Baylor, University of Texas at Austin, University of Indiana at Bloomington, University of British Columbia at Vancouver, University of Massachusetts at Amherst and Catholic University in Washington, DC. For many years, he has been associated with the summer programs at the American Institute of Musical Studies (Graz, Austria), Aspen Festival, Finnish National Opera (Helsinki), Teatro de Bellas Artes (Mexico City), International Institute of Vocal Arts (Franklin, NC; Tampa; Chiari, Italy and Miami Beach), Israel Vocal Arts Institute (Tel Aviv), Wolf Trap, (Vienna, VA), The Banff Arts Center (Banff, Canada) and others.

In addition to this book, Mr. Castel is currently involved in preparing a compendium of translations of all operas with phonetic transcriptions, to be published over the next several years by Leyerle Publications.

Mr. Castel lives in New York with his wife, Carol Castel, the noted stage director, is still at the Metropolitan Opera in his dual capacity, and is a judge on many panels that hear young singers. He still performs, and at times sings recitals that include many of his favorite Spanish and Ladino songs.